Victoriously Frazzled

The Frazzled Female's Guide to Restoring Her Sanity

Cindi Wood

LifeWay Press®
Nashville, TN

ISBN 1-4158-3202-1

This book is a resource in the Personal Life subject area of the Christian Growth Study Plan. Course CG-1205

Dewey Decimal Classification: 248.843
Subject Headings: WOMEN \ CHRISTIAN LIFE \ STRESS (PSYCHOLOGY)

Cover Illustration: Karine Daisay

Unless otherwise noted, all Scripture quotations are taken from the Holman Christian Standard Bible®, copyright © 1999, 2000, 2001, 2002, 2003 by Holman Bible Publishers. Used by permission. Scripture quotations identified AMP are taken from The Amplified® Bible, copyright © 1954, 1958, 1962, 1964, 1965, 1987 by the Lockman Foundation. Used by permission. *(www.lockman.org)*. Scripture quotations identified NIV are taken from The New International Version © International Bible Publishers 1973, 1978, 1984. Used by permission. Scripture quotations marked CEV are from the Contemporary English Version Copyright © 1991, 1992, 1995 by American Bible Society. Used by permission. Scripture quotations marked NKJV are from the New King James Version. Copyright © 1979, 1980, 1982, Thomas Nelson, Inc., Publishers.

To order additional copies of this resource: WRITE LifeWay Church Resources Customer Service; One LifeWay Plaza; Nashville, TN 37234-0113; FAX order to (615) 251-5933; PHONE (800) 458-2772; ORDER ONLINE at *www.lifeway.com*; or VISIT the LifeWay Christian Store serving you.

Printed in the United States of America

Leadership and Adult Publishing
LifeWay Church Resources
One LifeWay Plaza
Nashville, TN 37234-0175

Contents

Cindi Wood

Cindi Wood is an author, speaker, conference leader, and founder of Frazzled Female Ministries. She presents her Frazzled Female seminars for Christian women at luncheons, retreats, rallies, Bible studies, and a variety of other settings. She is the author of *I've Used All My Sick Days, Now I'll Have to Call in Dead*; *The Frazzled Female* trade book; and *The Frazzled Female* Bible study.

Cindi has also been involved in stress management training and related seminars for school systems, government agencies, state conferences, and corporate events.

Cindi earned a degree in intermediate education from Gardner Webb University in Boiling Springs, North Carolina. She has accumulated over 20 years of experience working with teachers, students, business leaders, and corporate administrators, helping them learn how to combat stress by managing time, developing a sense of humor, and learning to organize.

In recent years Cindi has felt the clear call to focus her experience and abilities on ministering to Christian women who, in spite of their faith, still feel overwhelmed, stressed out, frazzled, and in need of fresh hope and enthusiasm. Cindi's passion is to help women discover that a growing intimacy with Jesus Christ is the key to dealing with all areas of life—including the daily stress that often gets the best of us.

Cindi lives in Kings Mountain, North Carolina, and is actively involved in ministry at First Baptist Church. Cindi is a wife and mother of two sons. She enjoys exploring life with best friend-husband, Larry. Son Brandon is married to Bonnie and son Lane is married to Meghan.

To find out more about Cindi's ministry or to schedule a conference in your area, contact *frazzledfemale.com* or Regal Ventures Creative Ministries at 1-800-282-2561.

About the Study

Welcome to *Victoriously Frazzled!* Before you begin your study, let's look at some of the components. If you studied *The Frazzled Female,* the format will be familiar to you.

Victoriously Frazzled contains five weeks of content study and one week of reflection and commitment. Week 6 is designed to allow you the opportunity to process what you have learned throughout the study. All too often we come to the end of a Bible study and just put the workbook on a shelf without really reflecting on what the Lord taught us through the study. My prayer is that week 6 will help you do this.

Each week of study has a memory verse. I encourage you to memorize it during the first day of study and meditate on it throughout the week. Each week also includes a Defrazzler. This element will help you experience more deeply the concept you are studying that week. You may want to keep these strategies in place long after your study is complete.

The Relax in the Word section is an optional time of study. It is a time for you to just be with Jesus, studying the Word and relaxing in His presence. Don't feel guilty if you don't have time for this every week. You may need these times more some weeks than others. Be sensitive to the Lord's leadership when you sense He is guiding you into this portion of the study.

> "Draw near to God, and He will draw near to you."
> **James 4:8**

The daily sessions are designed to take 15 to 20 minutes, although you may spend much longer if you desire. The learning activities provide a time of reflection about how the study relates to you. You may be asked to express your feelings about things. These reflections may also be topics of discussion as you come together weekly with your small group to share what God revealed to you during your study. I strongly encourage you to complete all the learning activities to get the most from your study.

You'll need a pen, highlighter, and index cards to write your Scripture memory verses. Keep a notebook or journal close to jot down thoughts the Holy Spirit reveals to you as you study. You will also be encouraged to journal about some of the Defrazzler and Relax in the Word activities.

Are you ready? The sooner you get going, the sooner you can become "victoriously frazzled"! God bless you in your study!

Frazzle-Friendly

Memory Verse

"He who dwells in the secret place of the Most High shall remain stable and fixed under the shadow of the Almighty" (Psalm 91:1, AMP).

Defrazzler

Our God is a frazzle-friendly God! Not only will He enter into our stressful circumstances, He longs to be there to bring His relief, comfort, and joy.

This week you're going to have a fun defrazzler! Plan a SPA DAY! Whether it is an hour, an afternoon, or an entire day, do something to pamper yourself.

Need ideas? Manicure, pedicure, massage, facial, bubble bath, foot soak—something you never take time for or seems too luxurious to even think about. Your Heavenly Father longs to delight your heart and wants you to take care of yourself. You are royalty. You belong to the King!

Relax in the Word

Take some time during the week to relax while you read Psalm 139. Think about how you are "fearfully and wonderfully made." Thank God that He planned you long before you were born. Thank Him that He knows every-thing about you and still loves you. Worship Him and enjoy His presence in your life.

Day 1 Be Still and Let God Fight!

📷 **Focus:** Being still and allowing God to take over

📖 **Scripture:** Prayerfully read Exodus 14:1-14. Ask God to speak to you about His steadfastness when you are stressed.

"I can't take anymore!" Danita said as she flopped down in the recliner in her den. It was late afternoon, and plenty of evening duties still lay before her. She felt like she'd been putting out fires all day long with no one to help. Somewhere inside she knew she shouldn't be feeling so irritated and helpless. She was running out of energy and not enjoying life the way she used to. She breathed a prayer of *Lord, please help me,* but it was more out of desperation than a sincere cry for help!

Read the statements below and check all that apply to you.
- ○ 1. I have never felt like Danita.
- ● 2. I feel like Danita on many days.
- ○ 3. Most days I'm perfectly peaceful.
- ● 4. I used to feel stressed, but not anymore.
- ● 5. My life feels out of balance.
- ○ 6. Life is not as joyful as it used to be.
- ● 7. I need a body and soul makeover!

GOD WILL FIGHT OUR BATTLES!

"He lifted me out of the slimy pit, out of the mud and mire; He set my feet on a rock and gave me a firm place to stand." Psalm 40:2, NIV

If you checked numbers 2, 5, 6, 7 (or maybe ALL of them), then take heart frazzled sister! Your God is strong and mighty to save, and He's longing to invade your daily circumstances and pull you out of the pit (see Psalm 40:2)!

Only God can bring stability out of the messes of life. He loves for you to call on Him when you can't take it anymore. As your Heavenly Father, it delights Him to comfort you and rescue you! He understands your stress and how the events of daily living can leave you haggard and depleted. Sometimes living can take the life out of you, can't it? If you will turn to Him and allow Him, He will fight your battles, restore your joy, and usher you into victorious living!

What is your battlefield? Circle all that apply.

husband	work	caring for parents
housework	children	finances
illness	relationships	being on the go all the time
other _____		

Check the statement(s) that are true for you.

- ● I want God to fight my battles.
- ○ I don't know how to let God fight my battles.
- ○ It's hard for me to believe God can and will fight my battles.
- ○ I'm ready to try anything.

GOD HAS A PLAN

I'm intrigued by the story of Moses leading the Israelites in Exodus 14. God instructed him to turn them away from Canaan and lead them toward the Red Sea. This action would lead Pharaoh to think they were confused and just wandering around. God orchestrated this event, however, to bring glory to Himself! As Pharaoh and his army pursued the children of Israel, it appeared that God's chosen people were doomed. The Israelites thought so themselves. Instead of trusting, they cried out to the Lord and complained to Moses, telling him it would have been better for them to serve the Egyptians than die in the desert! But Moses, full of God's vision, encouraged and comforted them with the assurance of God's deliverance. "The Lord will fight for you; you need only to be still" (Exodus 14:14, NIV).

What appeared to be total chaos was not! It was God's plan to bring glory to Himself. His children were not faithful in believing that the same God who had always taken care of them would do it again.

Are you "an Israelite," wandering around doomed to stress and forgetting your God is in control and will lead you to victory?

In the battles you are facing, what do you need the Lord to do? Choose from the phrases below to fill in the blank on page 9.

provide peace	make things happen
take care of my situation	provide His strength
fight my battle	take care of my worries
watch after my family	resolve this problem

THE LORD WILL _Fight_ **FOR ME. I NEED ONLY BE STILL.**

What action will you take to allow God to fight your battles?

Believe and trust in God.

Write Exodus 14:14 on an index card or piece of paper. Carry it with you as a reminder that God has promised to take care of whatever is causing you anxiety.

GOD IS WAITING FOR YOU TO BE STILL

As a small child I escaped to the deep end of the pool one day and jumped into water way over my head. I remember fighting underwater, trying to get back to the top. The harder I fought, the deeper I went. I didn't know how to swim to the top. Exhausted, I stopped fighting and expected to drown. Still and helpless, I then floated to the top, where a rescue team was quick to pull me out.

Does this sound like you and a circumstance you are facing? Are you struggling, doing everything imaginable to "fight" whatever you're going through only to find yourself feeling exhausted and helpless?

Be still, my friend. Empty your heart of its anguish and toss out your battle-worn emotions. Cease your frantic thoughts and actions of desperation. Stop fighting and ease into the arms of your Savior who is waiting to rescue you.

> "I am at rest in God alone; my salvation comes from Him. He alone is my rock and my salvation, my stronghold; I will never be shaken."
>
> **Psalm 62:1-2**

What is God revealing to you through today's study?

The pleasures and I can have, by letting go and let God fight my battles.

As you close today's study, start your prayer time with this prayer:

Dear Father, I don't know how to be still. I've fought for so long; it's just my nature. I do believe that You want to fight this battle for me. Teach me, Lord. Show me how to be still in You. I trust You. I love You.

Day 2 The Secret Place

📷 **Focus:** Discovering special moments with Jesus

📑 **Scripture:** Read Psalm 91. Take your time, asking your Heavenly Father to reveal the truth about His love for you.

> "He who dwells in the secret place of the Most High shall remain stable and fixed under the shadow of the Almighty."
>
> Psalm 91:1, AMP

One day last winter it was raining, and I was stuck inside on the treadmill. I often use my exercise time to memorize Scripture. On this particular day I placed my wrinkled index card with Psalm 91:1 before me. Two words lodged in my heart. For the next hour, I could not get "secret place" out of my mind! It was as if God was romancing my heart with that concept. I did commit that Scripture to memory, but more importantly I committed my heart to a deeper intimacy with Jesus Christ by discovering more about the secret place.

Has God ever captured your heart with a certain Scripture? ◉ yes ○ no

If yes, describe your experience. After working so many days in a row, then they ask "can you stay an extra 4 hours. and when certain situations arise, I think about God says " he will supply All my needs, according to his riches and glory.

WHAT IS THE SECRET PLACE?

The secret place is a special place for only you and God. It's emotional, mental, and physical. It may be a place of joy. It may be a place of tears. It's a place where you meet your Savior in the crevices of your heart. And all who go there have a different experience. The secret place is reserved for God's children who have invited Jesus Christ to live in their hearts as their personal Lord and Savior. And even then, it's reserved for only the ones who desire it with their whole being. It's the depth of Jesus.

When you go there, you long to stay there. And if you've been there, you understand that all the words in this world could never describe the joy, peace, and fulfillment you experience being so close to Jesus. It's not a mysterious place in the sense of having to work your way through a maze to get there, but it IS mysterious in that the depth of Jesus is unexplainable and indescribable.

Have you experienced moments of being in the secret place? ○ **yes** ○ **not yet**

If so, how would YOU describe it? _____

_____

If you don't feel you've had this kind of depth with Jesus Christ, it's okay. You can experience a deeper intimacy with Him if you want to. I'm not trying to make the secret place sound like something magical, but it is supernatural. Paul talks about "secret wisdom" in 1 Corinthians 2:7. He goes on to tell how believers can understand God's truth because of the Spirit living in them. "We have not received the spirit of the world but the Spirit who is from God, that we may understand what God has freely given us" (1 Corinthians 2:12, NIV).

WHY DO I WANT TO GO THERE?

Several reasons come to my mind when I consider why one might want to go to the special place with the Lord. I've added Scripture references to show you the promises of God.

1 *I want stability in my life!* "[She] who dwells in the secret place of the Most High shall remain stable and fixed under the shadow of the Almighty!" (Psalm 91:1, AMP).

2 *I want to rest in God's peace instead of living in turmoil.* "Come to me, all you who are weary and burdened, and I will give you rest" (Matthew 11:28, NIV).

3 *I want others to see Jesus in my life.* "Let your light so shine before men that they may see your moral excellence and your praiseworthy, noble, and good deeds and recognize and honor and praise and glorify your Father Who is in heaven" (Matthew 5:16, AMP).

Choose one of these statements and claim the promise of that Scripture for your life. Briefly describe the reason for your choice. "I want to rest in God's peace instead of Living in turmoil". Because every time I think that my is out of the turmoil, and mess, here it comes again. and sometimes I would like to live with little stress, and in comfort.

HOW DO I GO THERE?

You understand what the secret place is. You want to grow your intimacy with your Savior. Now, how do you find that deep, abiding place with Jesus?

According to Matthew 4:18-22, which of the following statements about the first disciples are true? Check them.

- ○ They needed to do some things before following Jesus.
- ● They followed Him without delay.
- ○ They waited for a more opportune time to leave with the Lord.
- ○ They felt they didn't know Him well enough to follow Him.
- ○ They were willing to put all aside and follow Him.

You go to this deep and intimate place with Jesus by making Him your top priority. If you want to know Him more deeply, you can! And the way you learn about Him is to spend time with Him. It's simple in theory, but difficult in practice. You must be willing to put all aside and follow Him. The world will call you away. Satan will call you away. Your human nature will call you away. You must be determined to be obedient in your love for Him and your desire to know Him.

I often pray: *Lord, I don't know HOW to love You with all my heart and all my soul and all my strength. Will you teach me? Give me the desire to love you more!* It's then that Jesus seems to reach down, take hold of me, and assure me that if my desire is there, our love relationship will certainly grow as I meditate on Scripture and seek His face daily. And it doesn't matter if I grow this intimacy quickly or slowly. All that is important is that I'm growing it! The sweetness of taking those baby steps of loving Him is more than I can describe. Are you longing to grow your love for Jesus?

What is God revealing to you in today's study?

_____

_____

As you close your study time today, begin with this prayer:

Dear Father, I want to know more about the "secret place." I know You have wonderful things reserved for me in my love relationship with You. Teach me how to love You with all my heart, with all my soul, and with all my strength. I do love You, Jesus.

Day ❸ Sacred Balance

📷 **Focus:** Allowing God to balance your life

🔖 **Scripture:** Slowly read Romans 8:28-39. Ask your Heavenly Father to speak to you about His promise to balance your life.

Sandi loves the Lord, and she loves her family. There's no question about her love. What she does question, however, is how to make it all work—how to do it all, be it all, and experience joy in the middle of it all. She learned a long time ago to put the Lord first in her life, and she feels like she's done that. She reads her Bible on most days, goes to church every Sunday, and remembers to pray before meals. She knows her family is supposed to come next. She's worked hard on that one! Being very involved with each of her children's schedules, she's the ultimate I'm-here-for-you Mom. She has sacrificed her own pleasures, even her needs, to spend more time with her family. And now—with increasing demands at work and at home—she's exasperated and wondering, *How did my life get so out of balance?*

Single or married, children or none, young or old, whatever your status in life, you may be living totally out of balance. If so, you're likely feeling restless, maybe hopeless, and possibly defeated because of your circumstances. Rest assured, dear sister, God has something far better in mind for you!

Does your life feel out of balance? ⬤ yes ◯ no

Read the list of things that require your time and attention. Are you giving too much or too little attention? Are you balancing well? Circle your answers.

God	too much	too little	balanced
Husband	too much	too little	balanced
Children	too much	too little	balanced
Career	too much	too little	balanced
Home	too much	too little	balanced
Self	too much	too little	balanced
Church	too much	too little	balanced
_____	too much	too little	balanced
Other			

MORE THAN CONQUERORS

According to Romans 8:37, we are conquerors of our daily schedules—through Jesus. Regardless of the unbalanced mess you may find yourself in, you are ultimately the one in charge of your schedule. If there are things in your life that need extra attention, you need to back off some other things.

> "In all these things we are more than conquerors through him who loved us."
>
> **Romans 8:37, NIV**

Read each of the following statements aloud.
1. I cannot do everything.
2. I cannot be everything to everybody.
3. I will stop trying to do it all.
4. I will stop trying to be it all.

For reinforcement, write the statements below. THINK about what you are writing!

1. *I cannot do everything.*
2. *I cannot be everything to everybody.*
3. *I will stop trying to do it all.*
4. *I will stop trying to be it all.*

You were never meant to handle everybody's problems and take care of every situation that unfolds before you. It's unhealthy to even try. Women everywhere are juggling too many roles and finding insufficient time to do the things they are called to do.

DEFINING THE PROBLEM

Is there not enough time to do all you must do, or do you have too much to do? Sacred balance is evaluating your life by God's design and according to His plan. Consulting with Him is the only way I can balance my life.

At this time of my life, I'm a caregiver for my dad and my grandmom. I love them and love to take care of them. And I know it's a gift/responsibility from God that I do so. There are some weeks, however, that I don't feel like I give them adequate attention.

Obviously I can't spend all my time with them, and God doesn't want me to. Only He can tell me how to balance my time with them with the other things He is calling me to do.

Look back at the area(s) you indicated are unbalanced in your life. Have you talked with God about what you should do? ● yes ○ not yet

If not, pause and pray right now. Ask Him to impress upon your heart His plan to bring balance into your life instead of chaos.

What steps do you feel He is calling you to take to bring balance to your life?

sometimes we have to learn to let go of the very things, or persons that is causing our life unbalanced. so in simpler words, we need to let go and let God handle it.

JESUS IS INTERCEDING FOR YOU

According to Romans 8:34, Jesus is sitting at the right hand of God and interceding for YOU. He's praying for you to have a life that is balanced, healthy, and joyful. I must confess that I'm a bit frustrated because I know it's impossible to cover all the aspects of moving into a balanced life during these moments of study. But I don't have to cover it! God Himself is speaking to you! And He will continue speaking to you. Will you listen? Will you believe that if you ask Him, He will help restore the joy of your salvation and return you to a life of balance? I pray you will listen, believe, and experience!

> "Call to Me and I will answer you and tell you great and wondrous things you do not know."
>
> Jeremiah 33:3

What is God revealing to you through today's study?

_____

As you close today's study, start your prayer time with this prayer:

Dear Father, I long for balance in my life. I'm seeking Your face. Please impress upon me Your will for my life. I love You.

Day 4 God's Time Management Plan

> 📷 **Focus:** Learning how God wants you to manage time
>
> 📖 **Scripture:** Carefully read Malachi 3:1-10. Ask God to open your heart to how He wants you to manage your time.

A COMMITMENT TO GOD

The year was 1990. Once again I prayed, *Lord if you'll help me I will begin each morning with You. I love You and I want to be with You.* My prayer was sincere and my motive pure. I truly wanted to be with Jesus! So, with my plan in place and my Bible and journal by my side, I got up at 4:30 Monday morning. I decided that it was 4:30 in the morning or nothing. The baby woke up at 5:30. We were out the door by 6:30 headed for the baby-sitter for Lane, elementary school for Brandon, and work for me at the local middle school where I taught. It was the same pattern each morning. So, with my resolve to make it happen and my Bible in my lap, I fell asleep!

Oh, how Satan rushed in trying to defeat me and make me feel worthless! I'll never forget the way I experienced God's love at that time of my life. Instead of being consumed with guilt, I was overjoyed with how I sensed my Heavenly Father knew all about my tired body and my rigorous routine of being a wife, mother, and teacher.

Have you ever failed to keep a commitment to God? ● yes ○ no

If yes, how did it make you feel? *I felt real bad, because I WAS NOT BEING true to God and his word. Now, once I took care of that, I felt a whole burden lifted off of me.*

Do you think the feelings you experienced were from God? ● yes ○ no

Explain. *Because oneday I was at the 99¢ store, and gentlemen came up to me and ask me some change and I said that I don't have it, and all of sudden I hear this voice, saying to me that was not right." It saved me because nobody else was in the car, but me.*

SOME TIME WITH GOD

Some time ago I was preparing a workshop on time management for a conference of Christian women. As I studied and committed this event to the Lord, He placed a Scripture in my mind that I had learned as a child:

> "*Bring the whole tithe into the storehouse, that there may be food in my house. 'Test me in this,' says the L*ORD *Almighty, 'and see if I will not throw open the floodgates of heaven and pour out so much blessing that you will not have room enough for it' "* (Malachi 3:10, NIV).

I remember thinking, *Yes Lord, so?* Then I was zapped with what He was telling me. It was so exciting I couldn't write it down quickly enough: *Yes, this does have to do with tithing, but it also has to do with TIME!*

Has the Lord ever zapped you with a Scripture? ○ **yes** ○ **no**
○ **I have no idea what you're talking about.**

If so, what was it and what did it mean to you? _____

_____

You may not have a lot of time, but you do have SOME time. During the years when my children were young and my responsibilities included being a wife, mother, and teacher, I did not have a lot of time; but I did have SOME time to spend with God every day.

Check the statement that most nearly describes "where" you are in life.
   ○ I have sufficient time to spend with the Lord each day.
   ○ My time is divided between home, children, and other responsibilities; so I don't have a lot of time to have a quiet time with God.
   ○ I'm single but my life is overwhelmingly busy. I don't have much time to devote to a quiet time with God.
   ○ My responsibilities have shifted during the last years. I have more time to devote to growing my devotional and quiet time with Jesus.

If you don't have a lot of time, do you agree that you do have SOME time to spend with Him? ○ **yes** ○ **no**

I can't decide what's right for you. Nobody can. Neither is it profitable for you to compare the amount of time you spend in Bible study and prayer with anyone else. Only the Lord knows! And He alone is the one who will bless you for living in obedience to what He's calling you to do.

GOD'S MULTIPLYING PRINCIPLE

God said to the children of Israel, "Test me in this … and see if I will not throw open the floodgates of heaven and pour out so much blessing that you will not have room enough for it."

He's saying the same to you and me about our time with Him! God understands our schedules. He promises that if we will give Him some time—even if we only have a little time—He will take it and multiply our blessings because we are giving to Him in love and obedience!

My dear friend, are you beginning to understand how much God loves you and understands you? He's not asking the impossible, He's asking you to love Him and spend time getting to know Him deeply and intimately.

Knowing this, are you willing to offer—in obedience and love—to spend some daily time with Jesus? ⦿ **yes** ◯ **no** ◯ **I'll think about it.**

God will impress upon your heart how much time He wants you to spend quiet and uninterrupted with Him. It may vary from day to day. And it will probably change as the responsibilities of your life change.

Another verse that touched my heart while I was preparing for that session on time management was Hosea 6:6. "I'd rather for you to be faithful and to know me than to offer sacrifices" (Hosea 6:6, CEV).

Instead of growing my relationship with Jesus, I often substituted working for Him. He wants me to be *with* Him more than He wants me to do things *for* Him! That revelation has *so* deepened my walk with my Lord!

What is God revealing to you through today's study?

_____

_____

As you close today's study, start your prayer time with this prayer:

My dear Lord, create in me a heart full of love and devotion to You. Help me with my commitment to be with You on a daily basis. Show me Your time frame for my quiet time with You. I love You.

Day ✿5✿ Resting in Jesus

> 📷 **Focus:** Learning how to rest in Jesus in the midst of daily life
>
> 🔖 **Scripture:** Prayerfully read Mark 6:31, Psalm 57:2, and Philippians 3:10. Rest in the truth of these Scriptures as you meditate on them.

STUCK IN THE TRIVIAL

This e-mail from Gail got my attention!

> *My problems pale in comparison to what others are going through. I hesitate to even speak about them. I feel like they are so trivial—until I freeze and feel trapped, unable to create any movement in my life … I know God loves me. I know He wants to use me. I just don't see how He can.*

Have you ever felt this way? ● yes ○ no

If yes, explain. *Sometimes I feel that everytime I try to do something or get ahead in life, I get push back again.*

When I hear about tragedies that happen to others and major life events some are suffering through, I feel that my trials are so insignificant and so … nothing!

What we're experiencing at any given moment may not be as horrible as what others are having to endure, but the accumulation of little things can drive you nuts! Shout AMEN if you agree!

It doesn't matter why you freeze and feel trapped, unable to create any movement in your life, but it does matter that you feel that way!

NOTHING IS INSIGNIFICANT TO GOD

If it's about you, then it's important to Him! For some reason we have a hard time accepting that fact. We think our piddly little stresses don't matter to Him. Or, perhaps we feel guilty over the fact that we are bothered about them in the first place!

At a recent Frazzled Female retreat, I was speaking about how God wants us to talk to Him about anything that bothers us; anything that stresses us and robs us of our joy – ANYTHING! A young mother with three little boys came up to me during the break and said, "God doesn't want me to talk to Him about the way my boys scatter their dirty underwear through the house!"

What kinds of things have you felt were too insignificant to take to God?

_____

Does God want you to talk to Him about these things? Yes, He does! In Mark 6:31 Jesus says to us: "Come with me by yourselves to a quiet place and get some rest." You need to rest just as much from everyday living as you need rest and recovery from the major events of life!

Have you ever crashed because you didn't take the time to rest from daily living?
○ yes ● I always get plenty of rest.

CRY OUT TO GOD

I had finished the manuscript for the hardback version of _The Frazzled Female_ and was beginning on _Victoriously Frazzled_. Knowing the Lord had called me to this task, I was determined to get it done. On this particular morning I was overwhelmed with life and all the things that lay in my realm of responsibility. I cried out to the Lord saying, _Father, I know You want me to write this study for You. But Lord, You're going to have to do it for me. I can't!_

My Lord did what He's done time and time again. He rushed to show me His love and His encouragement. He literally placed before me my Bible that had fallen open to Psalm 57:2. Through tears, here's what I read: "I will cry to God Most High, Who performs on my behalf and rewards me—who brings to pass His purposes for me and surely completes them!" (AMP).

I have that verse taped to my computer for continual reference as I write. It's God's promise that He WILL complete what He has called me to do. I just walk in obedience step-by-step until it's done.

Can you think of a time when God rushed to show you His love and encouragement? If so, describe the situation.

_____

_____

MY DETERMINED PURPOSE

I've loved the Lord for a long time, but it's only been in recent years that I've embraced my love for Him as the goal of my life. Paul's words in Philippians 3:10 have helped me do this:

"My determined purpose is that I may know Him—that I may progressively become more deeply and intimately acquainted with Him, perceiving and recognizing and understanding the wonders of His person more strongly and more clearly" (AMP).

Having experienced His glory and His tremendous love for me through the trials of my life, there's nothing I want more than to know Him and love Him with everything in me! For me that's the ONLY way to completely rest! Plunging into Jesus restores my focus and my sanity. When life crashes in (which it often does), I just pull aside with Him to that quiet place and rest for a short while. In growing my intimacy with Him on a daily basis, I take baby steps toward my Savior, and those little steps produce BIG blessings. That's God's arithmetic!

It's not a method or a formula, but a relationship. God is a romantic at heart and He is calling you, His Bride, to enter into the most beautiful love relationship you could ever imagine. He's calling you that you may rest in Him while you live life here on earth.

"As a bridegroom rejoices over his bride, so your God will rejoice over you." **Isaiah 62:5**

What is God revealing to you as you close this week's study?

_____

_____

As you close this week's study, start your prayer time with this prayer:

Dear Savior, I long to enter into Your rest. I've never thought of You rejoicing over ME. Help me believe this truth. Teach me more about Your love and help me make the determined choice to grow my love for You. I do love You.

Control Freaks

Memory Verse

"Be completely humble and gentle; be patient, bearing with one another in love" (Ephesians 4:2, NIV).

Defrazzler

Choose a person or circumstance in your life that you feel a need to control. Now, back off for an entire week. Allow God to free you of this particular need to control. As you back off, pray for the person or about the circumstance. Consciously give your desire to control to your Heavenly Father. Allow Him to work things out. Be expectant and watchful. Notice what God does when you stop trying to control. During the week, write about your experience in your journal.

Relax in the Word

Take your time and relax as you read Galatians 5. Ask your Heavenly Father to speak to you about the freedom He has for you. Allow Him to speak to you about the fruit of the Spirit in your life. Enjoy this time to peacefully read His Word.

Day 1 Controlling Your Circumstances

📷 **Focus:** Learning to give your "control urges" to God

📑 **Scripture:** Open your heart to God's Word as you read and meditate on Acts 9:1-9. Ask God to bring to mind any area you seek to control.

GIVING IT TO GOD

The plane landed at 11:46. My connecting flight was four terminals away and departing at 12:01. Needless to say, I was a bit frantic as we touched down on the runway, visualizing myself sprinting through the airport to board the next leg of my flight. Armed with one big carry-on bag that had to be pried out of the overhead bin and one determined (if not stubborn) spirit, I barreled off that plane and set my gaze toward Gate 4D. Weaving through the crowd and trying not to take anybody out, I felt a nudge in my spirit saying, *You know, you're probably not going to make this one.* I remember a brief feeling of panic with that reality, but almost immediately I was flooded with His peace. I panted, "Lord I'm going to try my best to make it to that plane, but if I don't I know you have another plan."

How does being out of control make you feel? Circle all responses that apply.

anxious	confused	angry
helpless	sad	panicky
out of touch	regretful	other_____

STOPPED IN HIS TRACKS

Saul was a man who had his act together, and he was on a mission! Nothing deterred him from breathing those murderous threats and slaughtering countless disciples of the Lord. Nothing, except God Himself!

"As he neared Damascus on his journey, suddenly a light from heaven flashed around him. He fell to the ground and heard a voice say to him, 'Saul, Saul, why do you persecute me?' " (Acts 9:3-4, NIV).

Stopped in his tracks by God Himself, in a split second.

Describe a time you were stopped in your tracks, with all control taken from you.

_____

_____

Do you believe God was trying to get your attention? ● yes ○ no
If so, what do you think He was trying to tell you?

_____

_____

THE NEED TO CONTROL

By nature, I'm an organizer. When I organize it puts ME in control of my schedule, my circumstances, my day. At least that's the plan! So when things don't go according to my organizational plan, I get a little miffed. And when things get turned completely upside down (which happens more often than not in my life), I can get really stressed. I like to be in control!

I'm getting better at "allowing" God to order the events of my day. That's not to say I don't plan. It's just that when things don't go according to my plan, it's more okay than it used to be. God is teaching me that He wants to be in charge of all the ins and outs of my day. When the unexpected happens, He's teaching me to relax in Him and go with the flow, so to speak. It's not worth freaking out over. Besides, freaking out doesn't do one thing to help me regain control!

Do you need to "allow" God to have control of your day? ● yes ○ no

In what areas of your life do you need to hand over the reins? Underline them.

husband	work	children
housework	finances	friends
parents	schedule	church
community	other _____	

WHEN IT'S ALL SAID AND DONE

What helps me most in working through my control issues is remembering it's all about Jesus, not me! Galatians 2:20 helps me keep my focus.

And, by the way, I did catch that plane—just barely, but that was enough. I have a feeling God was using that opportunity to test my willingness to place my trust in Him instead of getting unnerved because I was no longer in charge.

That whole event was not about catching the next flight. It was about catching what God wanted to teach me: I don't have to be in control; He is! I'm celebrating that event because I passed a "control test." And I have a feeling He's going to send many more testing opportunities my way.

"I have been crucified with Christ and I no longer live, but Christ lives in me. The life I live in the body, I live by faith in the Son of God, who loved me and gave Himself for me." Galatians 2:20. NIV

What is God revealing to you through today's study?

_____

_____

_____

As you close today's study, start your prayer time with this prayer:

Dear Father, I know you want me to take control of some things in my life. I also accept the fact that I am not supposed to control everybody and everything. Help me know when to back off and submit to You and Your Authority. I want to experience Your peace in the control issues of my life. I trust You and I love You.

Day ✿2 Trusting God's Control

📷 **Focus:** Recognizing God's control

🔖 **Scripture:** Prayerfully reread Acts 1:1-9. Meditate on verses 5 and 6, asking God to give you a fresh meaning of these verses.

SOMETIMES OUR PLANS JUST DON'T WORK OUT

Andrea was chairman of the Walk for Those Who Can't event for her community. Even though she didn't feel equipped to pull it off, she agreed because she strongly felt God was calling her to head up this project. For months she and her coworkers had planned and strategized. They'd covered everything from food and sales vending to landscaping around the outdoor track. She felt at peace that everything was under control and everybody was cooperating—except the weatherman! His prediction of rain had her heart racing with panic.

She couldn't believe God would let it rain on this particular day. She had faithfully prayed over every committee member and every detail of her plans. It was God, after all, who had called her to do this, and she had agreed because she wanted to be obedient to His calling. Now the beginning of the walk was only hours away, and the forecast for the entire day was RAIN! Poor Andrea! Can you imagine her frustration and confusion?

Have you had a similar situation in which you gave your plans completely to God and then the unexpected happened? ○ yes ○ no

If yes, describe the situation.

_____

_____

Place an X on the continuum at the spot that best describes your reaction to the situation you just described.

1	2	3	4	5
No sweat				Full panic

"Who are you, Lord?" is the question Saul asked at that fateful moment of being struck down by God. I believe he knew who the Lord was. I think he was just reacting with a who-are-you-and-what-do-you-think-you-are-doing kind of attitude. I have no way of knowing that. I'm just basing it on how I've reacted to the Lord at times.

When I've committed my plans to Him in prayer and I've done my best to carry them through, I can't believe it when things go wrong! Are you like that? Have you ever been absolutely certain God would not allow something to happen and then the very thing you just *knew* wouldn't happen did?

How did you feel? Circle all that apply.

betrayed	confused	agitated
submissive	resentful	helpless
OK about it	peaceful	other _____

"I AM JESUS"

That was the reply Saul got. And that's the reply I get when I ask the Lord what He's up to when control is snatched away from me and things don't turn out the way I think they should!

Take your anger, frustration, confusion, and disbelief straight to Jesus when He allows your plans to go topsy-turvy. He knows how you feel anyway, and it's much healthier to lay it before Him than to keep stewing inside. God longs to fill you with His peace. He's not trying to get you rattled, but He may be trying to lead you to trust Him no matter how things appear.

The truth is, He is Jesus! He doesn't owe us an explanation. Many times I do not understand why He allows some things to happen, and why He doesn't seem to intervene in situations that are frustrating to me.

> God longs to fill you with His peace.

Are you frustrated because God doesn't seem to be intervening in a particular situation in your life? ◯ yes ◯ no

If yes, what is it you think He should do?

_____

_____

God allows circumstances in our lives that force us to give up control. While we may not have any control over the circumstance, we certainly have control over our response to it. I believe there's a critical response time. For me, if I immediately give it back to Him saying, "I don't understand Lord, but I trust You," I'm on the right track. If I keep company with disappointment and resentment, then it's more difficult for me to give back to God what is His.

How do YOU respond to God when things don't go your way? Check one.
- ○ kicking and screaming
- ○ trusting Him
- ○ some of both

TRUST IN THE LORD WITH ALL YOUR HEART!

It's a choice—and often a difficult one—to trust God when everything in life seems to be going wrong. Perhaps He's trying to get your attention like He did with Saul. Maybe He needs to "strike you blind" to get you to listen to Him. I've had a couple of those blinding experiences when it seemed God was getting right in my face and blocking out my surroundings so I'd get the message. I've decided to grow the practice of paying attention so He won't have to take such drastic measures to turn my attention to Him. If you forget that God is running the show, He'll certainly remind you!

Reflect on Proverbs 3:5-6 as you conclude today's study.

"Lean on, trust in, and be confident in the Lord with all your heart and mind and do not rely on your own insight or understanding. In all your ways know, recognize, and acknowledge Him, and He will direct and make straight and plain your paths" (Proverbs 3:5-6, AMP).

What is God revealing to you through today's study?

_____

_____

As you close today's study, start your prayer time with this prayer:

Dear Father, Thank you for being in control of all the circumstances in my life. Help me trust You more. Help me make the choice to trust You with all my heart and mind so that I won't feel I have to be in control. I love You.

Day ❸ Controlling the People in Your Life

📷 **Focus:** Seeking God's guidance about control issues

📑 **Scripture:** Prayerfully read Proverbs 4:23-27. Meditate on each verse, asking your Heavenly Father to guide you as you consider how these verses can affect your desire to control others.

EITHER / OR

When our son Lane was eight years old, our friend James was visiting in our home. "Dr. James" is a psychologist (we know how to pick friends!). One evening we were relaxing in the den and Lane scampered toward the back door saying, "I'll be back in at 8:15, Mom." For whatever reason, I thought his playtime outside should end at 8:00 instead. So the rest of the conversation went something like this:

Mom: "Be in by 8:00."

Lane: "Aw, Mom, just a LITTLE longer, please!"

Mom: "No, Honey. Be in at 8:00."

Lane: "Just a little longer. How about 10 minutes after 8:00?"

Mom: "Come in at 7:45 then."

Lane: "Okay. I'll be in at 8:00."

As he scurried outside and I felt a tiny smile of triumph tickle my lips, Dr. James asked, "May I make an observation?" Because he was such a good friend, he felt free to comment about how I interacted with my boys.

Always eager for free advice I said, "Sure, bring it on."

"Have you ever considered yourself an either/or person?"

"Explain what you mean."

Sparing you the psychological jargon, what he basically said was that Lane was allowed his playtime but it was either my way and on my terms or not at all. Maybe you've been like this, insisting it be done your way and in your time, and so forth.

Circle those with whom you have been an either/or person.

husband	friend	child	parent
coworker	sales clerk	other _____	

THE NEED TO CONTROL

There was great truth in Dr. James' observation. You may be thinking this was no big deal. Parents are entitled to have things their way and on their terms. And I agree, to a point. But there was no reason I couldn't have reasonably negotiated a few minutes more playtime. In that particular situation, it would not have been illegal, immoral, or dangerous. And it would have shown my son I was willing to take his desires into consideration.

To be truthful, that parent thing just kicked in and said, *you have to let him know who's boss and that you have the final word in EVERYTHING*. I came to realize there are times when I can allow my boys to have the final say.

Examining this issue of control in a new light, I considered these questions:

Why did I demand the boys' rooms be cleaned to my perfection?

Why did I insist they eat exactly what I gave them to eat?

Why did homework have to be done when I thought it should be done?

Why did I want to plan everything when my friends and I had a girl's day?

Why did it bother me when others offered to help in a project but didn't do things the way I thought they should be done?

OK, it's your turn. Give examples of your desire to control. You may experience "control urges" in all of these areas or only some of them.

job: _____

_____

home: _____

_____

vacation plans:_____

_____

relatives: _____

_____

church: _____

_____

holiday plans: _____

_____

committee meetings:_____

_____

other: _____

_____

BALANCE IS IMPORTANT

Sometimes our desire to control is within healthy limits. It's natural to want to be in control of your life and to have some control in the lives of others and the situations you encounter. But when there's an exaggerated emphasis on controlling people and situations, problems can certainly arise.

It's not healthy to be totally without control. Neither is it healthy or beneficial to be obsessed with control. God knows your heart and mind, and He holds the key to the balance between the two.

Where would you rank yourself on the compulsive controller scale? Mark your response on the continuum.

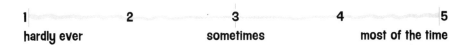

1	2	3	4	5
hardly ever		sometimes		most of the time

What is God revealing to you through today's study?

_____

_____

As you close today's study, start your prayer time with this prayer:

Dear Father, Please reveal to me any areas of control that are out of balance in my life. I love You.

Day 4 Positive Control

> 📷 **Focus:** Taking control of things I need to control
>
> 🔖 **Scripture:** Prayerfully read Esther 4:16–5:8. Ask God to reveal to you any area in your life where you need to take control.

ESTHER TOOK CHARGE

Esther made the choice to take control of a situation only she could address. The queen had been advised of a plot to kill all the Jews. If there were any chance of sparing them, she was the one to make that happen. She did not enter this situation without fear and trembling. For any person, including the queen herself, to enter into the King's presence without being summoned meant certain death. Only if the King found favor with her at that moment would her life be spared. Esther was willing to take this move on behalf of her people. "If I perish, I perish" (Esther 4:16). With great courage, this beautiful Jewess queen boldly entered into the throne room and presence of her husband, a temperamental pagan king. Because of her faithful willingness to boldly take charge, her life and the lives of God's people were spared.

Describe a time when it seemed you were the only one to take charge of a situation.

_____

_____

BEING IN CONTROL

So far this week we've explored negative controlling tendencies. There are many times, however, when we need to be the one in control. How do you know the difference? Which people and situations should you control and which people and situations should you not control?

First, let's examine the characteristics of the obsessive controller and the balanced controller.

Obsessive Controller	Balanced Controller
fueled by fear	realizes someone needs to take charge
seeks to control things to keep from being overwhelmed with anxiety	analyzes the situation
often feels helpless	takes time to think, pray, and act in obedience
appears not to trust others	realizes God is ultimately in control

Place an OC by the things you tend to be obsessive about controlling. Place a BC by the areas where you tend to be more balanced in control.

_____ friends   _____ meetings at church   _____ husband

_____ housework   _____ children   _____ meetings at work

_____ siblings   _____ other _____

SELF-CONTROL IS A FRUIT OF THE SPIRIT

"The fruit of the Spirit is love, joy, peace, patience, kindness, goodness, faith, gentleness, self-control" (Galatians 5:22-23). God begins to develop self-control in you as soon as the Holy Spirit takes up residence in your heart. You don't have to muster it up, but you DO have to stop, think, and appropriate the power of Christ instead of reacting from your own natural tendencies.

> God begins to develop self-control in you as soon as the Holy Spirit takes up residence in your heart.

Esther feared for her life and had every reason to do so (see Esther 4:10-11). She then took time to stop, consider, wait, and plan her course of action. Based on Esther's response and from observing others who have experienced victories in this area, I am offering some guidelines for you to consider. Think of opportunities when following these guidelines would lead you toward the more godly response of practicing self-control.

1. Pause – Deep breathe and collect your thoughts. Instead of rushing into a situation, take time to think.
2. Pray Scripture – Focusing on God's Word will always lead you in the right direction. Jeremiah 33:3 gives us great hope. God will lead us if we just ask Him! "Call to Me and I will answer you and tell you great and wondrous things you do not know."

3. Seek counsel – There are times when it helps to have a sounding board. This may be a trusted friend or a pastor. Pray with this person. If God wants you to seek another's opinion, He will lead you to the right person.

4. Stand still – Sometimes the best way to take charge is to do nothing. "The LORD will fight for you; you must be quiet" (Exodus 14:14).

5. Move in obedience – After you've had time to consider and pray about the situation, move in the direction you feel God is leading. Be bold and confident, knowing you have sought His face through prayer, Scripture, and perhaps godly counsel. Trust Him to lead you along the way. Be attentive to His direction, moving step-by-step as He leads.

Think of a past experience in which you needed to exercise self-control. Which of these five guidelines was the greatest challenge for you?

_____

Why? _____

_____

Sometimes we must act immediately without opportunity to stop, think, and consult others. If you have spent time with Jesus daily, seeking His counsel and reading His Word, then I believe He will guide you in those split-second decisions. I can confidently say that for me He moves me in His will as I breathe a prayer and respond with Him on my mind.

What is God revealing to you through today's study?

_____

_____

As you close today's study, start your prayer time with this prayer:

Dear Jesus, I have so much more to learn about self-control. You are my Creator and You know all about me. Teach me, Lord. Help me to exhibit Your fruit of self-control in my life. Show me the areas in which I need to take charge and act in obedience. I love You.

Day 5 Others Who Control

📷 **Focus:** Learning how to deal with others who seek to control

🪶 **Scripture:** Prayerfully read Romans 12:9-21. Ask God to fill you with His love for those around you who seem controlling and unlovable.

Cassie was sick and tired of feeling like this. Darla was her friend; in fact, probably her best friend. But lately she was getting on Cassie's last nerve! They had been through many things during the years and always seemed so compatible. Often they'd cry through their problems, only to end up laughing and sharing the deepest intimacies of their hearts. There was no one who knew and understood Cassie the way Darla did. There had always been much comfort, compassion, and gentleness in the way they responded to each other. Recently, however, Darla had taken on a new personality—a personality that really rubbed Cassie the wrong way. Darla was insisting on having her way in all their interactions. She seemed to have an agenda in every discussion and was always calling the shots about everything they did. She had moved from a warm, intimate friend to a person who was insisting on her way, never considering Cassie's opinion. She was turning into an absolute control freak!

Circle the "control freaks" you have encountered in your life.

family member   coworker   someone at church
friend   other_____

UNDERSTANDING OTHERS WHO SEEK TO CONTROL

Most of us have been around someone who seeks to control the people and circumstances around them. To get along with these people, we need to take a look at what's behind this need to control. For many, close ties to a relationship or circumstances exacerbate controlling tendencies. When you care deeply about others, you want the best for them. And to the controlling person, that translates into telling people what choices they should make. If the controlling people are in the middle of circumstances that need attention, they may step up to the plate and take over. They feel their mission is to take charge, have the final word, and get things done right.

I'm not excusing this behavior. I'm just offering the probability that many people who seek to control have good intentions. When I realize that, it helps me be a little more tolerant of their actions and compassionate of their needs.

Think about the controllers you know. Which of the following fears could be behind their need to control? Circle all that apply. Fear of ...

failing	losing a loved one	losing control of life
getting old	the unexpected	not being needed
being misunderstood	the future	things turning into chaos
unhappiness	other _____	

OFFER COMPASSION

Anxiety almost always fuels the need to control. The person who controls may not always admit or even realize that. But by seeking to control other people and situations, the controller is warding off fears of being helpless or having their control taken away. As situations and people around us change, we can all become very vulnerable.

I remember when my older son, Brandon, first left home. As I helped him move out of the house and watched him drive off, my mind was racing with *Who's going to take care of him? Will he eat the right things? Will he keep his apartment clean?* It was very difficult during our initial phone conversations not to plague him with all the things I wanted to make sure he was doing. As he moved out, my control over many things in his life moved with him.

This jurisdiction of control can change in a heartbeat. When control issues are changed, we become extremely vulnerable to fears and anxieties about being found helpless, useless, and out of control!

"Show family affection to one another with brotherly love. Outdo one another in showing honor." **Romans 12:10**

Are you gaining a better understanding of the person who seeks to control?

○ yes ○ no

Pause right now and pray:

Father, open my spirit right now to Your leading. Create in me a heart that is kind and full of compassion to those in my life who are seeking to control. Teach me to be compassionate in my thinking and my actions toward them.

People seek to control for many reasons, and there are different types of controlling tendencies. I'm not a psychologist and couldn't possibly address the many facets of this disorder. I'm just a frazzled female experiencing more and more of those wonderful victoriously frazzled moments, through the power of Jesus Christ who lives in me. He is teaching me how to better love myself and how to better love those who surround me—even those who, to me, are difficult to love!

So I offer you some dealing strategies, based on God's love and compassion. Think about these guidelines in dealing with those "control freaks" in your life.

1. Be "Jesus calm." Controllers tend to generate a lot of tension. Keep your distance (physically and emotionally) so that you can stay focused when you speak to them. Your calm body language and speech will help them stay calm, too.

2. Choose your words. The normal tendency is to speak rapidly and loudly when you speak to those who are trying to get the upper hand. Deliberately slow your rate of speech and carefully choose your words. This will have a calming effect on you and the other person.

3. Practice patience. Controllers need to be heard. Let them vent. Show them with your facial expressions that you care about them. Offer a few words to let them know you've heard what they've said. Remain calm until they've finished.

4. Be kind. Pulling this piece of artillery from your arsenal will have unbelievable results. While the other person is building those defenses of anger and lashing out, offer nothing but kindness. There's nothing like kindness to jam up a full-fledged verbal attack.

What is God revealing to you through today's study?

_____

_____

As you close today's study, start your prayer time with this prayer:

Dear Father, How I long to be clothed in the compassion of Jesus. It's only Your Spirit who can respond with love and kindness to those people who truly annoy me. Help me to know that in offering Your compassion, I am not justifying their actions. I'm just sharing Your love. Help them to notice. I love You.

Responding God's Way

👄 Memory Verse

"Whatever you want others to do for you, do also the same for them" (Matthew 7:12).

☢ Defrazzler

This week's defrazzler will not only help you experience joy in the Lord, it will directly affect the lives of others. Shock some people with a smile and greeting. Go beyond the formality of "How are you?" to something like "Great to see you today" or "Hi! Are you having a good day?" or something that fits the situation. It may be the person taking your dry-cleaning, a teller at the bank, or your server in the restaurant. Ask God to show these people the joy in your life. When they comment about how happy you are, have a response in mind. I often say, "I am happy because the joy of the Lord is my strength." Have fun with this one. Let it be a special sharing between you and God. I guarantee He'll place people in front of you who need an extra blessing, and you'll be blessed too!

☂ Relax in the Word

Enjoy reading through Romans 8. Ask God to speak to you about living life through the power of His Spirit. Remember that because of Him there's nothing you can't conquer in this life. He is your strength and you'll never be separated from His love.

Day 1 Reacting Versus Responding

📷 **Focus:** Becoming aware of what causes you to react negatively

🔖 **Scripture:** Prayerfully read Luke 8:22-25. Take time to meditate on the strong and calm composure of Jesus.

Jan was leaving the grocery store, juggling three bags of groceries and a sack of guilt. All she could think was *I wish I had handled that differently!* She felt absolutely horrible! In fact, she felt pretty bad before she ever made it to the store. She hadn't slept well for days. So her nerves were already on edge when she rounded the corner and was hit head-on by the cart of an oncoming speed demon. Jan, usually easygoing and calm, screamed, "What is your problem?" Immediately her spirit crouched in shame as the older gentleman replied, "Forgive me, ma'am. My wife just got out of the hospital. She's in the car and I was afraid to leave her, but I had to pick up a few things for supper tonight. I shouldn't have been in such a hurry."

Have you ever felt horrible because of the way you reacted? ◯ yes ◯ no

If yes, what happened? _____

_____

WHAT CAUSES YOU TO REACT

Some people just have a reactionary nature. But for many people who react in an explosive manner, contributing factors lead them to that volatile moment.

The same stress overload that weakens your immune system, making you more prone to sickness, also weakens your resolve to respond to situations in a Christlike manner.

Mark an X at the spot that best represents how you have tended to react to unexpected stresses during the past three months.

1	2	3	4	5

no reaction   **over the top**

Check the factors you think contribute to making you reactionary.

○ not getting enough sleep
○ hungry because of dieting
○ worried about something
○ stressed over all I have to do
○ grumpy because I don't have any help
○ feeling out of shape
○ nerves on edge from dealing with so much
○ family is uncooperative
○ house is dirty
○ other _____

Life has a way of wearing you down! It's difficult to keep your cool when everyone and everything seem to be going against the flow. When you don't feel well and nobody seems to be listening to you and life in general feels pretty rotten, it's difficult to respond with the gentleness of Jesus.

HOW DO YOU LEARN TO RESPOND?

How do you learn to respond like Jesus? You plan to. You think about situations ahead of time that could cause you to lose control and you pray about those people and events. You make yourself aware of where you are on your personal stress scale. If you're weighing heavy on the stress side, you may want to avoid some situations or people, if possible, until you feel calmer. And if avoiding isn't an option, you talk to the Lord about it. If you ask Him, He WILL help you remain calm and respond with His gentleness.

Because I am around people more often than not, and because I tend to use a LOT of words during any given day, I keep Psalm 141:3 before me and pray it often!

"Set a guard over my mouth, O LORD; keep watch over the door of my lips."
Psalm 141:3, NIV

Can you think of a recent situation that could have been handled in a more Christlike manner if you had prayed this verse before you reacted? ○ yes ○ no

Explain. _____

_____

POWER UNDER CONTROL

When I think of the gentleness of Jesus, I think of power under control. When He rebuked that fierce windstorm in Luke 8, He exhibited great power. But it was controlled power, not power running rampant. His words were well chosen, clearly spoken, and under control. What happened next? The storm subsided and all was calm.

Oh, how I long to respond like Jesus! Because of Jesus living in me, I can be assertive—not aggressive. I can respond on the spot with power under control.

God wants us to respond with His gentleness even more than we want it! He will help us if we pause long enough to think about Him and consider His calmness before we speak (or scream).

What is God revealing to you through today's study?

_____

_____

As you close today's study, start your prayer time with this prayer:

Dear Lord, I need Your gentleness and power under control as I deal with

this person: _____. I need Your gentleness and power

under control in this situation: _____

_____

_____

I love You.

Day 2 The Tongue of the Wise

> 📷 **Focus:** Learning to respond like Jesus
>
> 📖 **Scripture:** Take time to read Proverbs 15. Ask the Lord to use this passage to instruct you about growing godly response patterns.

GODLY RESPONSE

A crowd gathered for a Christian music festival. With the music growing louder and the temperature growing hotter, one person in the crowd began dancing wildly and annoying those around him. Adam moved in and tapped the young man on the shoulder, asking him to calm down. Without warning, the guy spun around and sucker-punched him, bloodying his nose. Adam steadied himself, regained his composure, looked his attacker squarely in the face, and said, "Hey man, this is a Christian concert and you're not acting very Christian. It's time for you to leave." Within moments, the security personnel escorted him away.

Adam is only 21 but has the spiritual maturity of one who has walked with the Lord for many years. Because of a godly response during an emotionally explosive moment, he was a tremendous witness for Jesus.

I want to be like Adam when I grow up! I am so impressed with the power of Jesus in his life. That kind of power doesn't just happen. It's not humanly possible to respond with the love of Jesus unless He lives in your heart and you've spent time with Him learning His ways.

Have you ever observed someone responding (instead of reacting) with the love of Jesus? ○ yes ○ no

If so, describe the event. _____

_____

HOT-TEMPERED VERSUS CALM SPIRIT

A calm spirit makes all the difference in a volatile situation. When emotions are unstable and events are unpredictable, it's easy to move into the defensive mode. And for me that means short words and jerky reactions. In my natural state I'm prone to a quick temper. It's taken years of prayer and dependence upon the Lord for me to learn to breathe in His presence before I jump into fight mode. Each time I take a deep breath and draw on the strength of the Lord instead of lashing out, I thank Him for the victory! This kind of growth does not happen overnight, but through a step-by-step process; and each step is worth celebrating!

> "A hot-tempered [woman] stirs up dissension, but a patient [woman] calms a quarrel." **Proverbs 15:18**

Have you noticed more godly response patterns in your life the longer you've walked with the Lord? ○ yes ○ no ○ haven't thought about it

In what situations or with which people have you noticed the most improvement?

_____

_____

If you are noticing improvement in the way you respond, celebrate the victories. Pause and thank the Lord right now.

REMINDERS ARE HELPFUL

It helps me to surround myself with reminders when I'm trying to learn a new skill. Months ago during my quiet time with the Lord, He revealed a change I needed to make. It had to do with a negative thought pattern. Since it was a skill I had not yet mastered, I needed frequent reminders to change my way of thinking. As a reminded, I chose to wear a little black band as a ring. All during the day when I noticed that little band, I remembered to apply my new thought pattern.

The same principle can be used for learning how to respond like Christ. If we don't think before we respond, and if we don't train ourselves to be like Christ, then we won't be like Him and we won't respond like Him. We need reminders placed in our paths to help us remember our goal.

When our children were little I made a banner of Proverbs 15:1.

> "A gentle answer turns away wrath, but a harsh word stirs up anger." Proverbs 15:1. **NIV**

That verse hung on our kitchen wall for years as a prominent reminder to respond to each other with love and gentleness instead of angry words. It wasn't decorative and it wasn't an impressive piece of artwork, but it was certainly a beautiful truth that we tucked deeper into our hearts and minds each time we noticed it. I'm so thankful God has given us reminders in His Word. I'm also thankful He has placed us in a world that contains many reminders from Him.

Below are some items that could serve as reminders to help you grow like Jesus. Circle the ones that might be useful to you.

sticky notes	a piece of jewelry	vase of flowers
framed Scripture	listening to a particular song	tied ribbon
an article of clothing	other_____	

SHARE ACCOUNTABILITY

Find a friend who will encourage you and hold you accountable to responding like Jesus. Share your concerns and your vulnerabilities with her. Allow her to pray with you and for you as together you grow in the Lord.

> "The tongue of the wise commends knowledge, but the mouth of the fool gushes folly."
> Proverbs 15:2, NIV

Do you have an accountability partner?
○ yes ○ no   If no, list in your journal or on a separate sheet of paper names of possible accountability partners. Pray that the Lord will connect you with the person with whom He wants you to build a relationship.

What is God revealing to you through today's study?

_____

_____

As you close today's study, start your prayer time with this prayer:

Dear Father, I long for those around me to see You in me. Please help me to pause and pray before I react to the situations I face today. I know You will help me if I ask You. Thank You. I love You.

Day 🌸 3 When Life Drives You Crazy

> 📷 **Focus**: Taking on the characteristics of Jesus during hectic times
>
> 🔖 **Scripture:** Prayerfully read 2 Corinthians 3:7-18. Consider the power available to us through the New Covenant, Jesus Christ.

MANIFESTING JESUS

I share the following story with great humbleness of spirit and some difficulty. For a long time, I couldn't speak about it for fear someone might think I was placing favor upon myself. But after a while I realized the manifestation of Jesus was so incredibly beautiful that the story needed to be shared.

A couple of years ago our son was in a tragic automobile accident which without the power of Jesus would have left him helpless and hopeless. Our mighty God miraculously healed all of Lane's body: a brain that had shifted and was hemorrhaging, a pelvis broken in four places, and lungs that had suffered trauma. We continue to praise God and adore Him for what He did!

Another miracle occurred during those first hours, and it happened inside of me. I had just returned home from a 5:30 a.m. workout when we received the call about the accident. I can look pretty rough early in the morning, especially if I've been exercising. And the news of my son's injury left me more haggard and disheveled than I had ever been. During the next 24 hours my physical appearance rapidly deteriorated, but the glory of the Lord exploded! Time and again, strangers walked up to me remarking, "You are so beautiful." I really don't know exactly what they were seeing, but I KNOW how I looked! I had been physically worn down, and the beauty they were seeing was the beauty of the Lord!

Have you ever been aware that God showed His glory through you? ○ yes ○ no

Did you have trouble believing He was manifesting Himself in YOU? ○ yes ○ no

We *should* be humbled, in awe, and thankful, but not surprised!

"We are therefore Christ's ambassadors, as though God were making His appeal through us" (2 Corinthians 5:20, NIV). We are "Jesus in the flesh" to a world who does not know Him. We can encourage our brothers and sisters who do know Him with His love and His constant presence in our lives.

We know the Lord is with us and a part of each event we live through, so it should never surprise us when He manifests Himself through us.

In which ways have you noticed the manifestation of Jesus in another person? Circle them.

facial expression   words spoken   body language

behavior   godly response   silence

other _____

Describe an event where you witnessed the manifestation of Jesus in someone.

_____

Did you tell that person you saw Jesus in him or her? ◯ yes ◯ no

TAKE OVER, LORD!

When things are going smoothly in life, it's easy to shine the love of Jesus, isn't it? The real test comes when life is driving you crazy and that sinful nature kicks in. You know—that nature that's filled with worry, anger, fear, and STRESS! That's when "the world" is really watching, especially unbelievers. They're looking to see if our walk matches our talk. They're searching and hoping that Jesus does make a difference, because they're not too sure about the whole Christianity thing. During those times, God makes His appeal through us.

When do you think God is most likely making His appeal through you?
◯ when things are calm and peaceful
◯ when I am happy
◯ when things are not going well
◯ during a crisis
◯ when I am worshipping
◯ other _____

NEW COVENANT, NEW CREATION

According to 2 Corinthians 5:17, because of Christ living in me I'm a new creation! I like the word *new*. It makes me think of things fresh and untarnished. That's exactly who we are in Jesus! If Jesus lives inside of you, then you are in a position to reflect His glory.

I can position myself to reflect the glory of Jesus to the world around me by allowing the Lord to transform me into His likeness. The Lord does the transforming. That's His plan for us through Christ Jesus. He gives me the choice, however, to cooperate with His plan.

"We all, with unveiled faces, are reflecting the glory of the Lord and are being transformed into the same image from glory to glory; this is from the Lord who is the Spirit." 2 Corinthians 3:18

Do you want the Lord to transform you into His likeness? ● yes ○ not sure

If yes, to what will you commit? I will cooperate with God's plan by:
- ○ daily reading His Word
- ○ becoming more aware of His presence in my surroundings
- ○ talking with Him throughout my day
- ○ inviting Him to be a part of all the details of my life
- ○ worshipping Him as I work around the house
- ○ thinking about Him as I run errands
- ○ thanking Him and acknowledging His presence in my life
- ○ other_____

Circle the areas in which you long for God's transforming power in your life.

interaction with my family	running daily errands
being out in public	in my voice
in my facial expressions	in being a caregiver
at work	when life smacks me in the face
answering the telephone	other _____

What is God revealing to you through today's study?

_____

_____

As you close today's study, start your prayer time with this prayer:

Dear Lord, I want to be a worthy ambassador for You. I want You to freely manifest Your glory through me. Show me how to grow more deeply in love with You so I may experience Your transforming power in my life. I love You.

Day ❹ When Others Are Unkind

📷 **Focus:** Being like Christ when others aren't

🏷 **Scripture:** Carefully read Matthew 7:1-12. Think about how Jesus treated others. Pray that God will give you the perspective of Jesus.

Janice stopped by the store to pick up a few things after work. It had been a hectic day and she felt tired and grumpy from dealing with stressful situations. Walking into the store she passed Susan, who chaired the social committee at church. When Susan noticed her, instead of greeting her with a smile and a "hello, friend" she quipped, "Have you turned in your idea for the table decorations? They were due last week, you know." Janice, already irritable because of her hard day at work, paused. Instead of snapping back, she caught her breath and slowly said, "Thanks for the reminder. I'll do that when I get home."

Have you ever been caught off guard by someone snapping at you? ⭕ yes ⭕ no

If yes, describe how you felt at the time. _____

_____

I DIDN'T DESERVE THAT

"You have heard that it was said, Love your neighbor and hate your enemy. But I tell you, love your enemies and pray for those who persecute you."

Matthew 5:43-44

I can think of more than a few times when someone spoke harshly to me and I didn't feel I deserved it! Sometimes I caught myself, like Janice, and responded in a calm manner. Other times I quickly retaliated. I am always more pleased with *me* when God gets the glory through a calm and kind response on my part.

Check all statements that are true for you.
- ○ I've been the recipient of harsh words.
- ○ I probably deserved the rebuke.
- ○ I did not deserve the rebuke.
- ○ I responded calmly and kindly.
- ○ I retaliated with harsh words.

When I think of *enemy* I think of one who has an ongoing hostility towards a person or a cause. I believe in the context of the Matthew 5 verse, however, that your friend who acts unkindly and abruptly could even be your enemy—at least at that moment. Jesus instructs us to be filled with love and to pray for anyone who persecutes us.

"If your enemy is hungry, give him food to eat, and if he is thirsty, give him water to drink; for you will heap coals on his head, and the LORD will reward you." **Proverbs 25:21-22**

HEAPING COALS

The idea of heaping coals on my enemy's head has always intrigued me. I believe Jesus is saying if your enemy is hungry and thirsty tell him you're sorry, but then go the extra mile and give him food and water. That extra mile, so to speak, is the heaping of coals! The way to turn an enemy into a friend is to be friendly to him.

Think of a recent situation when you were treated less than kindly. Briefly describe the scenario. _____

_____

What could you have done to "heap coals"?
- ○ smiled and changed the subject
- ○ invited the person to go to lunch
- ○ shared a Scripture verse
- ○ written a note of encouragement
- ○ offered my help
- ○ other _____

Proverbs 25:22 tells us that if we heap those coals, the Lord will reward us! I can't think of a better reason to bite my tongue and lay my spirit down before another. I long to be rewarded by Jesus. And the greatest reward I receive is the realization that I have pleased Him in my attitude and behavior.

If you can just get by that split second of injury—the moment of your attack—then you have the blessed opportunity of honoring Christ and experiencing a special token of His presence. Remember my story about Adam and the sucker-punch from Day 2? I can imagine the angels in heaven giving high-fives when that young man faced his attacker in kindness instead of punching him back. What a Jesus-empowered moment and one that will be rewarded in heaven! The earthly reward is the joy of honoring Jesus in the here and now.

Today you have the opportunity to honor your Lord by righting a wrong, repenting of a wayward attitude, and laying aside your feelings for the cause of Christ.

Spend some time in prayer with your Heavenly Father. Ask Him to reveal to you a past situation that needs His healing touch. Ask Him to show you what you can do to share His love and bring honor to His name.

When He has brought a situation to mind, consider how you will bring honor to Him. Check the commitments you will make.

- ○ I will write a note.
- ○ I will make a phone call.
- ○ I will initiate a conversation.
- ○ I will pray for this person and about this situation.
- ○ I will seek God's guidance about what He wants me to do.
- ○ I will keep this person or situation before the Lord until I sense His peace.

What is God revealing to you through today's study?

_____

_____

As you close today's study, start your prayer time with this prayer:

Dear Father, Grow me to be like Jesus. Help me want to treat others the way You would treat them. Give me Your love for all the children You created. I love You.

Day 5 Reactions Worth Having

> 📷 **Focus:** Intimacy with God brings godly reactions
>
> 📖 **Scripture:** Read Judges 4:1-16; 5:1-3. Reflect on the confidence of Deborah as she spoke and moved in the strength of the Lord.

Deborah was a prophetess and judge for the nation of Israel. She also went to war with them, bringing Israel to victory and leading them in praise to God for the deliverance of His people. Deborah was quite an impressive woman. She spoke God's command to go into battle to the commander of the army, Barak. He reacted with fear and cowardice. But Deborah moved forward, standing shoulder to shoulder with Barak on the battlefield. When the commander of the army wavered, Deborah stood strong in her faith, trusting God to do what He said He would do, even though the odds seemed stacked against Israel. When victory was certain, Deborah reacted with gratitude and an overflowing heart full of praise. Her musical thanksgiving lifted the spirits of the Israelites and ushered them into praise to God for the greatness of His power.

GODLY AND APPROPRIATE REACTIONS

This week we've explored negative reactions that cause harm and inflict hurt. There are times, however, when reactions can have a positive effect.

One afternoon while walking through her neighborhood, Jean passed an acquaintance who lived several blocks away. She noticed the woman was teary-eyed and moving slowly. Immediately Jean gave her a hug and asked if she could help. She could have walked on, spoken while ignoring her emotional state, or turned and walked the other way. Jean's godly reaction was to respond affectionately to her neighbor. As a result, Jean was able to share some comforting words.

Have you ever reacted in a godly way to someone in need? ○ yes ○ no

If yes, describe what happened. _____

_____

Was the person helped because of your reaction? ○ yes ○ no ○ not sure

STEEPED IN GOD

I pray that I will be so steeped in Jesus that when those opportunities come to share His love, I'll move right in. I do believe it's very important to breathe a quick prayer before the approach! When there's not time to bathe a situation in prayer, the Lord will impress upon you what to do, if you ask Him. Only He knows the person, the situation, and how He wants you to react.

> Not reacting when He doesn't want you to is just as important as reacting when He does want you to!

Go back to the story about Deborah. Circle the phrases that describe a reaction. Then fill in the following blanks.

Barak reacted with _____ **and** _____.

But Deborah _____ _____, **standing shoulder to shoulder . . .**

When the commander of the army _____,

Deborah stood _____ _____ _____ _____ . . .

Deborah reacted with _____ **and an overflowing heart**

_____ ____ _____.

I believe Deborah was able to react in a godly way because she was so steeped in God's presence. If you spend time with Jesus on a daily basis, you will begin to take on His characteristics. You will begin to think like Him, behave like Him, react like Him. It makes sense that if you saturate yourself in the Scriptures and the presence of God, you will be more likely to react like He would in any given situation.

When life's stressors come flying my way, I'm very aware when the grace of Jesus takes over. It's like a touch to my spirit before I speak or move. It's so NOT like me to be calm and serene in the middle of haphazardness. But the more time I spend with Him, growing my love for Him, the more I become aware of His presence throughout my day.

Can you recall a time when you reacted graciously in a situation that normally you would not have handled well? ○ yes ○ no

How would you explain this reaction? _____

_____

We've spent five days exploring how to react like Jesus. The best way to train yourself to do so is to spend time with Him on a regular basis. Spending time in prayer and in the Scriptures equips you in ways no earthly method can. Talk to your Heavenly Father about it. Ask the Holy Spirit to speak your words, move through your body, and shine on your face. These qualities will attract the world around you to Jesus, and those are reactions worth having!

> "The good man brings good things out of the good stored up in his heart … for out of the overflow of his heart his mouth speaks."
> Luke 6:45. NIV

What is God revealing to you through today's study?

_____

_____

As you close today's study, start your prayer time with this prayer:

Dear Father, You created me to live in this world, and it's normal for me to have reactions to the people and situations around me. I want Jesus to shine in my expressions and the words I speak. I love You.

Experiencing God's Practical Power

☙ Memory Verse

"Come with me by your[self] to a quiet place and get some rest" (Mark 6:31).

☢ Defrazzler

This week you are going to run away with Jesus! As bizarre as that may sound to you, I want you to entertain the idea and even get excited about your retreat time! Jesus is calling you to a quiet place with Him—to get some rest! Sometime this week pull away from your daily activities and draw close to Jesus, being aware of His presence and thinking about how He longs to have time alone with you. You may choose to have a candlelit snack, inviting Him to join you as you thank Him and reflect on His love. You might take a walk, leisurely shop, or simply sit quietly and meditate.

It's important to schedule times periodically when you can experience an extended time with Him, focusing on His presence and love. There's power to be found in this quiet place! I know it will be a challenge for you to schedule this quiet time in your busy week, but I encourage you to give it a try and "taste the goodness of the Lord" (Psalm 34:8).

☂ Relax in the Word

Take some time this week to kick back and relax with an old, familiar passage. Read and meditate upon the love of your Shepherd as you slowly work your way through Psalm 23. Be still before Him. Praise Him. Enjoy Him. Allow Him to restore and refresh your soul. Sometime during the week, journal about your experience.

Day 1 God Loves to Surprise Us!

> 📷 **Focus:** Expecting God to call your name
>
> 📖 **Scripture:** Open your heart to God's word to you in 1 Samuel 3. Imagine Him calling your name, just as He called the name *Samuel* in this passage.

CAUGHT OFF GUARD BY GOD!

Have you ever had the experience of God speaking to you in an unlikely circumstance? Kaye has. "When my husband wants to get my attention, he uses this certain whistle. And when he whistles, it seems I always hear him. It may be in a crowded room or when he is standing above me on another level of the shopping mall or above the endless chatter of our two boys. Even though he doesn't whistle loud, it always gets my attention. One day I was walking in our neighborhood. I was praying and very burdened about some problems I was experiencing. All of a sudden I heard 'the whistle.' This may seem weird, but I knew immediately I had heard the whistle in my heart from my loving Heavenly Father, telling me to put my attention on Him and know He would take care of me."

Has God ever spoken to you in a way the world would consider weird?
○ **yes** ○ **no**

If yes, underline the words or phrases that best describe how you felt.

surprised	fearful
excited	curious
doubtful	wanting to hear more
full of joy	crazy
expectant	other _____

Briefly describe your experience.

_____

_____

HEARING GOD'S VOICE

Not only was young Samuel caught off guard by God's voice, he didn't even recognize it was the voice of God speaking. First Samuel 3:7 says that "the word of the LORD had not yet been revealed to him." Verse 1 tells us "the word of the LORD was rare and precious in those days" (AMP).

Some time ago I went through a period when it seemed God was distant and I couldn't "feel" His presence or sense His nearness. I knew He was there, but I wasn't experiencing the closeness with Him that I had once experienced.

Have you ever felt distant from God? ○ **yes** ○ **no**

If yes, how did you respond?
- ○ talked to a pastor or friend
- ○ spent more time in prayer
- ○ spent more time in Bible study
- ○ asked God why He seemed far away
- ○ felt guilty
- ○ wrote about my feelings in my journal

We go through times of feeling distant from God for many reasons. One of the most powerful lessons I have learned through these trying times is that I must never base my relationship with Jesus solely on my feelings. If I do, my feelings will tell me He has betrayed me and I know that will *never* happen!

If you are experiencing a time when God seems far away, I encourage you to keep pressing on! Keep seeking His face through the study of His Word and keep that private, personal love relationship alive by worshipping Him throughout your day. Ask God to reveal and remove any barriers to your relationship with Him and to bring you back into close fellowship with Him. Cry out the psalmist's plea from Psalm 51:12, "Restore to me the joy of Your salvation" (NIV). Be faithful and diligent in your love life with Jesus and your joy will return.

I KNOW WHAT ELI KNEW

Upon realizing it really was God speaking to Samuel, the old priest, Eli, helped position Samuel to hear God's voice. In other words, he alerted Samuel to the fact that God was speaking to him and told him to simply respond to the voice, saying, "Speak, LORD, for Your servant is listening" (v. 9).

Perhaps you, like Samuel, need to be told (and reminded) that God is speaking to you. Allow me to be your Eli. I want to tell you that God loves you and is pursuing a love relationship with you. And He wants you to hear His voice and welcome Him into your daily life of places to go, things to do, and people to take care of.

> God loves you and is pursuing a love relationship with you.

What is God revealing to you in today's study?

_____

_____

As you close today's study, start your prayer time with this prayer:

Dear Father, Thank You so much for desiring to have a love relationship with me. Help me, Lord, to love You with all my heart and all my soul and all my mind and all my strength. Help me to hear You calling my name, and then help me to listen to what You say. I love You.

Day 2 THE EBENEZER STONE

> 📷 **Focus:** Remembering God's help in the past
>
> 📖 **Scripture:** Read 1 Samuel 7:3-12. Ask God to help you remember times when He has helped you during difficult circumstances.

I just love what took place in 1 Samuel 7:12! After the Israelites smoked the Philistines, Samuel set up a stone, calling it *Ebenezer*, meaning stone of help. He did this as a visual reminder for the Israelites, so they would remember how God fought and won that battle for them.

That was an unlikely victory (humanly speaking) for Israel, but God rushed in and did His thing—the very thing only He could have done! God rushed into the middle of a terrible circumstance and exploded His victory!

Have you experienced a time when God intervened in an unlikely circumstance and showed His glory? ○ yes ○ no

If yes, how did you feel?

○ surprised   ○ thankful   ○ joyful
○ stunned   ○ nervous   ○ undeserving
○ relieved   ○ overwhelmed   ○ loved
○ other_____

Briefly describe the circumstance.

_____

_____

How was God glorified in this event?

_____

_____

MY OWN EBENEZER STORY

While writing *The Frazzled Female,* I experienced some really stressful times. God used those stressful times to affirm in me that He is indeed the Author of peace, joy, and stability during the crises of life.

Remember the story about our son Lane's car wreck and the miracle God performed in his body? The words Jesus spoke concerning Lazarus in John 11 certainly rang true in that situation.

"This sickness will not end in death. No, it is for God's glory so that God's Son may be glorified through it."

John 11:4, NIV

To help us remember how God rushed to help us during that time, I clipped portions of the x-ray that showed the damage to Lane's body. We each have a small remembrance, a "monument of victory," reminding us to continue to praise Jesus for His help.

Do you have a "monument of victory" that represents a particular event in your life? ○ yes ○ no

If you do, describe it and how it helps you remember God's intervention.

_____

_____

COLLECTING EBENEZER STONES

A couple of months ago, while studying 1 Samuel, I was impressed to spend some time thinking back through my life about times when God seemed to rush to help me. I began listing these events in my journal. Each time I recorded one event, another one came to mind. As my list grew, so did my thankfulness! I experienced a fresh realization of the sweetness of Jesus. He so longs to be our Helper, our Strengthener, and our Comforter!

Recording those times when Jesus rushed to help me blessed my heart in a fresh new way. I want you to have the same experience.

Take a few moments to sit quietly before the Lord and make an "Ebenezer list" below. Use your journal or a separate sheet of paper if you need more space.

_____

_____

_____

_____

_____

_____

You may choose to complete your activity by doing something like what I have done. I collected polished and different colored stones. In my journal, I designated stones to stand for each event. Then I put them all in a beautiful little bag, calling it my Ebenezer bag. The collection of Ebenezer stones helps me remember to thank God for His help in my past, knowing He will continue to help me in my future!

What is God revealing to you through today's study?

_____

_____

As you close today's study, start your prayer time with this prayer:

Dear Father, Thank you so much for Your love for me and for Your help during the difficult times of my life. Help me remember to continually thank You for the many ways You help me through every day. I want to love You more.

Day 3 HOLY SPIRIT, I NEED YOU!

> 📷 **Focus:** Welcoming the presence and help of the Holy Spirit
>
> 🏷 **Scripture:** Slowly and prayerfully read John 14:15-29. Ask God to give you a fresh excitement about the presence of His Spirit in your life.

COUNSELOR

Laurie dreaded the phone call she had to make. For weeks she had struggled with the decision to put her grandmother in a nursing home. In order to reserve the room, today was the day she had to give her final answer. She had gathered her facts and felt she was well informed, but she still had that unsettling feeling of not quite knowing if this was the right thing to do.

In a flashback, she remembered reading in a daily devotional about the role of the Holy Spirit in giving guidance. She vaguely remembered where the passage was when Jesus said He would send His Spirit to help us. After some searching, she located these verses in her Bible. "I will ask the Father, and He will give you another Comforter (Counselor, Helper, Intercessor, Advocate, Strengthener, and Standby), that He may remain with you forever" (John 14:16, AMP).

That's it! She needed a counselor to help her make this decision. Did Jesus really mean that He would help her TODAY in making this decision about her grandmother?

Do you believe that the words of Jesus apply to us today?
○ yes ○ in some situations ○ no

Let's examine the Scriptures.

Read John 14:6,16-18. Fill in the blanks in these statements.

Jesus said, I am the _____, the _____, and the _____.
No one comes to the Father except through Me.

I will ask the Father, and He will give you another Counselor to be with

you _____.

The Spirit of Truth. The world cannot accept Him, because it neither sees

Him nor knows Him. But you know Him, for He _____
with you and will be in you.

DO YOU BELIEVE JESUS?

If you have accepted Jesus into your heart as the Lord of your life, then the
Holy Spirit has entered into a living relationship with you. He lives in you
and is constantly with you. And He *is* your Counselor, your Helper, your
Intercessor, your Advocate, your Strengthener, and your Standby!

**This activity will help you see where you need the Holy Spirit's help in your life.
Taking the names given to Him in John 14:16 (AMP), list areas in your life where
you need His guidance. In what situations do you need a:**

Counselor: _____

_____

Helper: _____

_____

Intercessor: _____

_____

Advocate: _____

_____

Strengthener: _____

_____

Standby: _____

_____

James 4:2 tells us that we do not have because we do not ask. We are also told that when we ask we can believe God is going to answer! (See James 1:6.)

WE CAN BELIEVE JESUS AND HIS WORD

The power of the Holy Spirit is available to us today. We must recognize that:
1. He lives in us.
2. He wants to help us.
3. We can ask Him for help.
4. We can believe Him.

Then follow up with obedience. He may lead you to carry through with something or not to do something. He may ask you to change your attitude about a certain matter or apologize to a friend. He may simply want you to thank Him for filling you with His peace and freeing you from worry.

I can't list all the ways He might speak to you, but I can assure you He will!

What is God revealing to you through today's study?

_____

_____

As you close today's study, start your prayer time with this prayer:

Dear Jesus, Thank you so much for the gift of Your Spirit. Forgive me for not always acknowledging Your Spirit's presence in my life. Right now I ask You to make me more aware of Your Spirit and teach me to ask You for specific help as I go through my day. I love You.

Day ❹ Speaking His Word

📷 **Focus:** Saying Scripture aloud

🔖 **Scripture:** Prayerfully read Philippians 2:1-11, asking God to draw you close to His Spirit and to help you be more like Jesus.

KAREN'S STORY

I met Karen in a remote little town in Virginia during a Frazzled Female retreat. What I saw happen to her and the power—the practical power—that was manifested in her still bring tears to my eyes. We gathered around to sing praise songs after supper on the first night of our retreat. I noticed that Karen was not singing and offered to share my praise music with her. She responded dryly, "I don't sing." Something in her countenance led me to be very troubled in my heart about that comment. Later that evening, Karen asked to talk with me. She shared about the troubling events going on in her life as well as difficult issues she had struggled with as a child.

"I don't sing" kept coming to my mind.

Excited and hopeful, I said, "Karen let's try something. I believe that God wants you to sing!" She looked at me with disbelief, becoming visibly annoyed. She had just poured her heart out to me, and I was talking to her about singing! I knew, however, what the Spirit had spoken to me and insisted that we try singing together.

I sang, "God, you're so good ..." and no Karen! She just looked at me as we held hands together, her eyes filling with tears. Finally, in the middle of sobs, she very quietly opened her mouth and began audibly praising God through song.

Do you sing your praises aloud to God? ○ yes ○ no

If yes, where do you sing aloud?

○ at church ○ at home
○ in the car ○ in the shower
○ at work ○ other _____

Circle the words and phrases that best describe how you feel when you sing aloud to God.

happy	fulfilled	embarrassed
worry free	grateful	appreciative of His love
at peace	silly	thankful
inadequate	humbled	overwhelmed
other _____		

Karen and I sang for the next 10 minutes. Karen began to laugh and cry. So did I. It seemed that I could see her being freed from bondage—emotional and spiritual bondage. She knew Jesus as her Savior, but was not speaking aloud His name in praise.

She shared this with me the following day: "You know, you were right about the singing aloud thing. I have been singing to God in my heart, but I needed to praise Him aloud. This has made all the difference in the world. I feel like I have been set free!"

That incident was a powerful testimony to me—a testimony of God's desire to "hear" our praise. It's wonderful to have the praise of God living in our hearts; but I believe it's a double-whammy aimed right at Satan when we shout His praise, sing His praise, or pray aloud the Scriptures, giving God audible credit for who He is and all He has done.

Have you experienced a time when you knew God wanted you to be verbal in praising Him or in repeating Scripture? ○ yes ○ no **Were you obedient?** ○ yes ○ no

Share your experience. _____

_____

_____

CONFESSING WITH YOUR MOUTH

Confessing means saying the same thing as or agreeing with. So, when you "confess with your mouth" praise to God through singing or reciting Scripture, you are verbally saying the same thing as God and agreeing with Him.

Confess with your mouth (say aloud) the following Scripture.

"I can do everything through Him who gives me strength" (Philippians 4:13, NIV).

Did you say it aloud? Say it two more times.

When I pray (confess) Scripture aloud, I often reword it, making it personal to me. Here's how this passage goes: "I can do everything through YOU who gives me strength."

"If you confess with your mouth, 'Jesus is Lord,' and believe in your heart that God raised Him from the dead, you will be saved. For it is with your heart that you believe and are justified, and it is with your mouth that you confess and are saved." **Romans 10:9-10, NIV**

Here's another example: "Do not throw away your confidence. It will be richly rewarded" (Hebrews 10:35, NIV). When I personalize it, it becomes: "I do not throw away my confidence because it will be richly rewarded."

Try your hand at putting these Scriptures in personal prayer form.

"He is my loving God and my fortress, my stronghold and my deliverer, my shield in whom I take refuge" (Psalm 144:2, NIV).

_____

_____

_____

"I consider that our present sufferings are not worth comparing with the glory that will be revealed in us" (Romans 8:18, NIV).

_____

_____

_____

Confess aloud Psalm 144:2 and Romans 8:18.

Determine to confess these verses aloud during the day today. You may want to copy them on an index card or slip of paper for easy reference.

Take some index cards and personalize some other Scriptures as you feel led. I'm finding that by reading them often and praying them aloud, memorizing them is much easier. In other words, when I pray Scripture aloud concerning a need I have in my life, the Scripture becomes personal to me.

What is God revealing to you through today's study?

_____

_____

As you close today's study, start your prayer time with this prayer:

Dear Father, Thank You for giving me lips to proclaim Your Word! Help me to confess Scriptures aloud during the day—knowing that I am speaking in agreement with You as I confess them. I'm excited about learning new ways to experience Your love. I love You.

Day 5 Early in the Morning

📷 **Focus:** Starting the day with Jesus

🔖 **Scripture:** Prayerfully begin your study time by reading Psalm 143. Ask your Heavenly Father to reveal Himself to you, showering you with His love and His provision for the day ahead.

FIRST THING IN THE MORNING

Leslie got up a half hour earlier than usual. She really wanted to draw closer to Jesus and experience His presence in her life more than she ever had before. Now, here she was at 5:30 a.m. with her Bible and her journal, ready to spend time with Jesus and she thought, "Here I am, but what do I do?"

Can you identify with Leslie? Maybe you have also wondered what to do during a quiet time with Jesus.

Below you'll find a list of some possibilities—some things people do during their quiet times with the Lord. Underline the ones you would be comfortable doing.

sing softly to Him	write a prayer to Him
read Scripture	play a musical instrument
thank Him	meditate on a specific Bible verse
kneel before Him	tell Him how much I love Him

Do you have a special activity you enjoy doing during your early morning quiet time? ○ yes ○ no

If so, what is it?_____

_____

DEVELOPING GODLY HABITS

One young woman in a recent Frazzled Female session commented, "I don't want my quiet time with Jesus to become just a habit!"

I understand that she meant she didn't want to have a quiet time that was done just to be done, with no meaning to it. But the truth is, we need godly habits in our lives!

Habits are behaviors that become routine because we do them over and over. Routine in the way of consistency in our spiritual life is very important! As we discipline ourselves to praise God, speak Scripture aloud, study the Bible—along with any other spiritual behaviors that we do consistently—we will create godly habits!

Doing something good one time does not produce long-lasting spiritual results. But doing it over and over until it becomes a godly habit in our lives gradually brings us closer to Jesus.

Circle the godly habits you already have in place in your life.

Scripture study	praying for others
confessing Scripture	thanking God
interceding for others	acknowledging the Spirit's presence
singing to God	journaling
having a quiet time with God	talking to Him throughout the day
other _____	

Go back and put a star beside those you would like to become habits.

EARLY MORNING CHECKLIST

When I first became serious about my quiet time with the Lord, I made a checklist on the first page of my journal so I would have a guideline to follow. You may find this procedure to be helpful as you begin committing this time to Him each day.

This list helped me develop a format to follow each morning. As time passed, I added some other things as well. But for the most part I still begin my days like this.

1. I pray Psalm 143:8: "Cause me to hear Your loving-kindness in the morning, for on You do I lean and in You do I trust. Cause me to know the way wherein I should walk, for I lift up my inner self to You" (AMP).

2. I spend time thanking Him. Often, I mentally go through the previous day, thanking Him for how He was involved during each event, conversation, errand, and so forth. I thank Him for saving me and for pursuing a love relationship with me.

3. I offer Him a repentant heart seeking forgiveness for specific sins and for missing the mark of holiness in certain thoughts and behaviors.

4. I welcome the present day ministry of the Holy Spirit. Asking Him to intervene in the specifics—whatever they are—in the day ahead.

Using the above list as your guide, make a checklist in the space provided on page 69 that will help you establish the godly habit of a quiet time with Jesus. Feel free to use suggestions I've given as well as those of your own. Be creative and ask the Holy Spirit to help you! He's your Guide and Counselor. He will help you create an early morning routine that will bring glory to God and blessings to you!

As you close today's study, dedicate your early morning time to Him.

Dear Father, I'm excited about growing closer and closer to You. Thank You for what You are teaching me and for the hunger You are placing in my heart. I give the days ahead to You. Awaken me each morning with a fresh excitement to enter into Your presence. I love You very much.

MY CHECKLIST

_____

_____

_____

_____

_____

_____

_____

_____

_____

_____

_____

_____

_____

_____

_____

I'm Getting Old!

💋 Memory Verse

"I will be the same until your old age, and I will bear you up when you turn gray. I have made you, and I will carry you; I will bear and save you" (Isaiah 46:4).

☢ Defrazzler

This week's defrazzler is going to be fun! Think of something fun you used to enjoy when you were a child. (I loved making mud pies!) Sometime during this week, do that fun activity. If it involves others, you'll have to solicit some help. This is a wonderful way to discover the child within you. Enjoy yourself. Laugh and play—it's a great way to celebrate life!

Ask your Heavenly Father to teach you more about the childlike qualities He wants you to have in your relationship with Him. Be sure to record your experience in your journal!

☂ Relax in the Word

Enjoy time with God as you read 1 Corinthians 13. Take your time. Focus on the content. Has your definition of "true love" changed throughout the years? Pray for your Heavenly Father to renew your love for Him. He loves you extravagantly. Ask Him to help you believe that!

Day 1 We're All Getting Older

> 📷 **Focus:** Being content with growing older
>
> 📖 **Scripture:** Read Ecclesiastes 3:1-11. Ask God to speak to your heart about the seasons of your life.

One day last summer, my son's girlfriend, Meghan, and I were sitting at the kitchen bar laughing and talking about the way things used to be. Meghan blurted out, "Gosh! I'm getting old." I laughed at her outburst. Being up almost three decades in addition to her two, I had to agree. Life indeed was forging ahead and taking us with it. Reflecting on that conversation for the rest of the day, I realized a truth hidden in Meg's words. Even though she was all of 20, she was expressing the sentiment of most females past their teens: *I'm getting old!*

What age were you when you first thought you were getting old? _____

How did this realization make you feel? Circle all that apply.

sad	surprised	excited	frightened
happy	intimidated	independent	inspired
confident	worried	depressed	other _____

IT'S A GOOD THING

Truth is, we are all getting older. With each month, year, day, and minute we are growing older! The good thing about growing older is that we *are* growing older! Even considering the parts of the body that droop, drag, and stretch, (not to speak of the things that disappear like well-toned skin and memory) there's much to be said about tucking experience under our belts and knowing more than we used to.

You have weathered some challenges that "girls" younger than you haven't yet experienced. Depending upon your age, you know some things about loss, learning by doing, the challenges of singleness or married life or raising children or not being able to have children, and more. You probably know more than your younger sisters from how God has helped you through rough times and the lessons you've learned by sheer faith and placing your trust in Him. Hopefully you have more wisdom, more stamina (spiritually if not physically), and more insight into the deeper things of life.

We all make statements based on age. Think of three you've used to show your "age clout." I've given my all-time favorite!

"You'll understand one day, when you're a mother."

1. _____

2. _____

3. _____

BEAUTIFUL IN HIS TIME

> "There is an occasion for everything, and a time for every activity under heaven."
>
> Ecclesiastes 3:1

"He has made everything beautiful in its time. He also has planted eternity in men's hearts and minds (a divinely implanted sense of a purpose working through the ages which nothing under the sun but God alone can satisfy)" (Ecclesiastes 3:11, AMP).

That's YOU. You are beautiful in HIS time! Whatever age you are, it's the right age for you right now. God has a purpose designed for you at this time of your life that is different from any other time of your life.

Much earlier in my life God placed in my heart the passion to teach women. The motivation was there. The desire was there. The longing was in place. The only element missing was opportunity! I gain so much insight by looking back on those years and reading my heart cries in my journal. I was confused and bewildered about why the doors of ministry were not opening. I knew God was giving me a dream, but I was totally confused about why it wasn't happening.

Now I know why it didn't happen right then. God's plan for me was to bump and bruise my way through some difficult tests and trials so I could be qualified for what I was about to teach.

God uses everything in your life to grow your experience, faith, and love for Him! And there's no other way to develop those qualities except growing through them and growing older. No matter your age right now, you are in the process of growing within God's plan!

Circle the areas where you feel more "qualified" because of life experiences.

singleness	divorce	death of a loved one
marriage	parenting	buying a home
moving	caring for parents	finding a career
serious illness	losing a job	other _____

PROCESS, NOT OUTCOME, GLORIFIES GOD

I believe we spend too much time thinking about the final goal and what's next, instead of focusing on the present. I had those tendencies even as a child. I remember my dad saying to me during our family vacation, "Enjoy what we're doing right now, instead of worrying about what we're going to do next!"

Often I sense my Father saying to me: *Where you are right now, this very moment, is what's important to Me. Don't worry about tomorrow and don't fret over yesterday. Don't focus on what's going to happen. Love Me now. Trust Me for this very day. Worship Me now and delight in Me now.* The key is NOW!

How does this apply to getting older? It seems to me our society overemphasizes the next phase of life, whatever that may be. For the child it's early adulthood. For the young adult it's mid-life; for the mid-lifers it's retirement. Please don't misunderstand. I'm not suggesting we not plan and prepare for what's next. I'm just saying we should enjoy the present!

What worries about another time of life (past or future) are robbing your enjoyment of the present?

_____

_____

What is God revealing to you through today's study?

_____

_____

As you close today's study, start your prayer time with this prayer:

Dear Father, Thank You for this time of life. Help me see Your plan for me. I want to glorify You in the experiences I have already had, as well as those still to come. I love You.

Day ✿2 Age and Body Image

> 📷 **Focus:** Developing a balanced view of your body
>
> 📑 **Scripture:** Read Matthew 6:25-34. Ask God to speak to you about the focus He wants you to have regarding your body.

A POSITIVE BODY IMAGE

"Stop being perpetually uneasy (anxious and worried) about your life, what you shall eat or what you shall drink; or about your body, what you shall put on. Is not life greater (in quality) than food, and the body (far above and more excellent) than clothing?" **Matthew 6:25, AMP**

There seems to be a direct correlation between the way we feel about our bodies and our self-esteem. Putting proper emphasis on taking care of our bodies is important. Notice I used the word *proper.* If we neglect our bodies as we journey through life, we'll suffer some real, negative physical consequences. But overindulging in things like exercise or dieting is not good either. The clothing we wear also contributes to our overall body image. This area can easily get out of balance as well. Do you get caught up in the latest styles, splurging on fashion trends, or are you more practical in your approach to what you wear?

I believe "perpetually uneasy" means placing the focus where Jesus does not want it to be. In other words, it's a good thing to think about what we eat, drink, wear, and how we exercise. But Scripture tells us we should never become obsessed with those things.

Have you ever been obsessed about eating, exercising, or clothing?
○ **yes** ○ **no**

Explain. _____

_____

What problems occurred because of your obsession? _____

_____

_____

THE PROPER VIEW

I enjoy exercise—well, mostly the benefits of exercise. But years ago I realized that I was overindulging in a good thing. I became preoccupied with running and weight training. Beginning with a healthy focus, I gradually placed too much emphasis on these activities. At some point, I crossed the balance line and was sprinting and toning my way to fatigue and obsession. Thankfully, I saw the warning signs and began to slack off this rigorous training program. Too much is just as unhealthy as too little.

Here are some strategies to help you find balance in your body image as you age.

1. Identify things you like about yourself that have nothing to do with your body. Maybe you have a great sense of humor or you're a great organizer or hostess. Build on those qualities.

2. Explore your emotions by writing about them in your journal. Focus on growing your positive attitude and ditching some emotions that are weighing you down, like worry or guilt.

3. When you look in the mirror, think of something NICE. Just as you are eager to compliment others in their appearance, find something you like about YOU.

4. Take stock of your exercise program. No exercise program? Begin one! Exercise is not only good for the body, it's good for the soul! Find something you like to do. Begin a program with a friend. Be creative about it. You can find ways to exercise—even during the busiest days—if you put your mind to it. Think of the time of day you would be most likely to stick to a program. If you hate mornings, then get some exercise at lunch or early in the evening. Many experts agree that 20 minutes of exercise four times a week is a good start. The discipline you build in this area will help you accomplish goals in other areas of your life.

5. It's YOUR decision. Be careful about taking the advice of everybody else. This is about you! Don't fall under the prey of well-meaning people who think they know what you should eat and how you should exercise or look. You know your own body better than anyone else.

TALK TO THE LORD

> "Seek first the kingdom of God and His righteousness, and all these things will be provided for you."
>
> Matthew 6:33

Your Heavenly Father is interested in every aspect of your life. He created your body, your mind, and gave you emotions and desires that are unique to you. He knows what areas need some extra attention. Ask Him! Let Him direct your feelings about your body and give you His take on the best exercise and eating lifestyle for you.

Ask Him to brighten your outlook about who you are and His purpose for you. He longs to answer you when you seek His face!

After talking to the Lord, circle the number of the balance strategy from page 75 that you feel you need to focus on.

1   2   3   4   5

What is God revealing to you through today's study?

_____

_____

As you close today's study, start your prayer time with this prayer:

Dear Father, You created my body. It's Your design. I know You want me to take care of my body. Please show me Your balance. Help me appreciate who I am in You. I love You.

Day ❸ Age and Attitude

> 📷 **Focus:** Being content with your present age
>
> 🔖 **Scripture:** Read Exodus 2:1-9. Think about Miriam's devotion to her baby brother as she boldly carried out her mission.

IS ATTITUDE EVERYTHING?

Grandma Pearl lives up to her name. At 97 she's indeed a rare and precious find, and continually delights me with her commitment to a positive attitude. Months ago, I walked into White Oak Manor where she lives AND leads the daily exercise program for the residents. The tables and chairs in the dining room were pushed aside, making it a workout floor for the next 20 minutes. With participants in a circle and my grandmom up front, the wheelchair aerobics began. I watched intently as everyone in that circle tried to exercise. I could see the commitment on their faces as they struggled to lift their arms and swing their legs. My grandmom was the perfect instructor, coaching each one to try her best and lift her limbs to whatever degree was comfortable. Their eyes danced as they swam in the ocean and tiptoed down the beach. Being the cheerleader on the sidelines, I was completely enthralled with what was taking place before me. Everything in me applauded as I scanned the faces of those dear ladies who were giving their all to perform each movement. When the routine was finally over, there was great celebration in that room. As they all sat back and relaxed, there was lots of laughter and sighs of victory. It all ended with my grandmom wrapping her arms tightly around herself and calling her comrades to do the same, saying, "Give yourself a big hug—you've done a great thing!"

Name an older person who has influenced you with his or her positive attitude.

_____

Share something special about that person.

_____

_____

USEFUL AT A YOUNG AGE

"His sister stood at a distance in order to see what would happen to him. ... Then his sister said to Pharaoh's daughter, 'Should I go and call a woman from the Hebrews to nurse the boy for you?' ... So the girl went and called the boy's mother."
Exodus 2:4,7,8b

In every age of life, we have opportunity to serve our Heavenly Father! His calling on our lives is not reserved for only a particular span of our lifetime. We have opportunity to glorify Him—whatever our age!

Miriam was a young Jewish girl under the care and teaching of her mother. She had been trained in the qualities of boldness, wisdom, and courage. In a timely act of faith, she stepped forward to the Pharaoh's daughter and asked the question that led to saving the life of Moses and the ultimate delivery of God's chosen people. "Should I go and call a woman from the Hebrews to nurse the boy for you?"

Useful at a young age? I would say so!

Think of a young girl who is making an impact for Jesus. How is she being useful? _____

_____

USEFUL AT AN OLDER AGE

"Miriam the prophetess, Aaron's sister, took a tambourine in her hand, and all the women followed her with tambourines and dancing." **Exodus 15:20**

As we move through the account written in Exodus, we continue to learn about Miriam's faithfulness in serving God. She became a strong female leader, accompanying her brothers and assisting them in the leadership of the Israelites. She had great influence, not only with the women who followed her, but with the entire nation of Israel as she helped point them toward God's promised land.

Think of a woman who is in her middle or older years of life. How has she inspired you with her usefulness to God? _____

_____

I thank my Heavenly Father for the women of all ages who are attending Frazzled Female events and going through the Bible studies. One commonality we all share is that no matter our age, each of us is getting older!

Most of the time getting older is just fine with me. Truthfully speaking, however, there are other times when I seem to have difficulty getting over getting older!

Are you ever bothered about getting older? ○ yes ○ no **Explain your answer.**

_____

Some promises in Scripture can help get us through these times when we have difficulty accepting that we are getting older.

He planned out every single day of your life before you were born! "Your eyes saw me when I was formless; all my days were written in Your book and planned before a single one of them began" (Psalm 139:16).

He is never closer to you than He is at this very moment! " I will be the same until your old age, and I will bear you up when you turn gray. I have made you, and I will carry you; I will bear and save you" (Isaiah 46:4).

Your body will change. Your appearance will change. Your ability to function will change. Your Jesus will NEVER change! "Jesus Christ is the same yesterday and today and forever" (Hebrews 13:8, NIV).

What is God revealing to you through today's study?

_____

_____

As you close today's study, start your prayer time with this prayer:

Dear Father, Thank You for being my constant companion through each stage of my life. Fill me with the awareness of Your presence as I move through the days, months, and years ahead. I want to be in love with You at every age. Oh, how I love You!

Day 4 Embracing the Moment

📷 **Focus:** Making the most of NOW

📑 **Scripture:** Read Matthew 7:7-28. Take your time and enjoy this reading, welcoming the truth God longs to reveal!

MID-LIFE CRISIS

Some of you have heard about it and have it to look forward to. Others have weathered it and gotten to the other side. Many of you are in the throes of that middle time of life that ushers in all sorts of new feelings, shaky expectations, and possible opportunities. I heard about it long before I got here, and I'll be sharing about it long after I leave. Everybody I know has (or will have) a mid-life crisis story. Here's what's going on with my 45-year-old friend, Pat:

With her third daughter getting ready for college, Pat has shifted her focus from soccer games, proms, and late night vigils to exercise and competition. She's embracing this new time of life as an opportunity to take better care of herself and improve her health. She's also enjoying the rush of running in races and accomplishing goals she never even thought of setting. With a twinkle in her eye, she tells me, "It's just my mid-life crisis!"

Describe a mid-life event that you or someone you know has experienced.

_____

_____

BEARING FRUIT

The good tree bears good fruit; the bad tree bears bad fruit. The age of the tree is not mentioned in Matthew 7:17. You know why? It doesn't matter!

Think of two women you know who are bearing good fruit. Fill in the blanks.

Name _____ Age _____ Good Fruit _____

Name _____ Age _____ Good Fruit _____

Sometimes I hear people make excuses because of age, as if the infirmities that happen along the timeline of life give us excuses not to bear good fruit. I fully believe that if you're a Christian it is God's design for you to bear fruit at every age of life. True, there may be limitations of being too young, too old, or too inexperienced. But we are not called to bear ALL the good fruit, just the good fruit He is calling us to bear.

Name two age-related excuses you've heard for not enjoying life and bearing fruit.

1. _____

2. _____

I've heard way too many women use hormones for an excuse, along with aches and pains that give way to griping and complaining because of age-related illnesses. I've come to the conclusion that old crabby women were young crabby women. They're not crabby because they're old; they're crabby because they're crabby!

Now, before I get this page yanked out of this study by my editor, let me explain. My intent is not to be judgmental or critical of anyone who suffers physically, emotionally, or even hormonally. Suffering hurts! I've been through many pain-filled days with a body that just couldn't handle any more and emotions that were fried.

My goal is, through the love of Jesus, to lead you to assess where you are right now. Are you using conditions in your life to keep you from experiencing His love and bearing His fruit? My 97-year-old grandmother could easily have used aches and pains and the inability to walk as an excuse not to lead that exercise program. If she had, nobody would have blamed her. But since she didn't, many women have experienced a special blessing of exercise.

CLINGING TO THE ROCK

Aging can be downright depressing! If you approach it from a worldly sense, you're apt to sink down in despair as those years creep on. The years are still coming, though, unless you leave this world first!

But the good news is indeed good. In fact, it's freeing and exciting! With Jesus Christ in your heart, you can face each and every day with fresh excitement because He *is* your excitement. He longs to give you energy for each new day and a new passion at each stage of life! You can embrace life—like my friend Pat—with new and constructive energy to live life in a different way.

"The rain came down, the streams rose, and the winds blew and beat against that house; yet it did not fall, because it had its foundation on the rock." **Matthew 7:25, NIV**

Pause and pray. Ask God to fill you with new excitement so you can embrace the season of life you're in right now!

The truth is, dear friend, unless Jesus lives in your heart and rules your mind and emotions, your "house" will shatter to pieces. Each stage of life presents new and potentially destructive challenges. At each stage of my life there have been difficult physical, emotional, and mental challenges. Without clinging to the Rock, I would be much more battered and bruised than I am today.

Check each statement that applies to you. Because of Jesus I have:
- ○ been able to work through frantic emotions.
- ○ jumped the hurdle of disappointment.
- ○ made it through financial difficulties.
- ○ experienced peace when the rug was pulled out from under me.
- ○ sensed His presence in unlikely circumstances.
- ○ been restored after a season of sin and guilt.
- ○ not been left helpless and hopeless.
- ○ other _____

What is God revealing to you through today's study?

_____

_____

As you close today's study, start your prayer time with this prayer:

Dear Father, I long to experience Your goodness, and I want to bear good fruit for You. Help me not make excuses because of the limitations of my age. Help me set and accomplish the most important goal of all—building my foundation on You. I love You.

Day 5 Life to the Fullest

📷 **Focus:** Understanding the meaning of "growing up"

📖 **Scripture:** Prayerfully read Philippians 3:7-16. The Lord longs for you to experience life to the fullest. Ask Him to show you how.

WHEN I GROW UP

I've often heard my friend Janet remark, "I want to be a ballerina when I grow up." I smile every time I hear her say it. She is a school administrator and even thinking of working on her doctorate. She loves her work and is quite content in it. And yet, there's a longing somewhere deep down to have a simpler lifestyle—one that embraces the joy of living and self-expression.

Are you like Janet? Is there someone you'd like to be that you never got to be? Is there something you'd like to do that you never got to do?

Here are some secret goals women have shared. Circle the ones you've thought of or make a list of your own. Some day I would like to:

sky dive	write a book	climb a mountain
visit another country	jet-ski	go on a cruise
perform on stage	get a degree	plant a garden
paint a picture	play the piano	give a speech
other _____		

MATURING

One of the definitions of *maturing* is becoming fully developed and perfected. That's how I like to think of growing older. It sounds more noble and even classy to realize I'm developing and moving toward perfection instead of getting old!

Paul hit it right when he said, "Not that I have already obtained all this, or have already been made perfect, but I press on to take hold of that for which Christ Jesus took hold of me. [Sisters], I do not consider myself yet to have taken hold of it. But one thing I do: Forgetting what is behind and straining toward what is ahead, I press on toward the goal to win the prize ... all of us who are mature should take such a view of things" (Philippians 3:12-15, NIV).

Part of this "moving toward perfection" is letting go of past regrets. Whether it's regretting things done or things left undone, there's simply no reason to hang on to them. You have no opportunity to relive and redo yesterday's moments, but you do have every opportunity to do it right now.

Do you ever struggle with regrets over the past? ◯ **yes** ◯ **no**

Has anything beneficial come from dwelling on them? ◯ **yes** ◯ **no**

LET YOUR SCARS BE REMINDERS, THAT'S ALL!

Five years ago I had neck surgery that left a three-inch scar on my throat. I tried every ointment and miracle cream I could find. I could not make it disappear. As months and years passed, it faded but was still there. Gradually I made peace with it. Instead of looking at it now with disgust, I see it as a reminder of a time when God truly helped me keep my sanity in the midst of physical pain!

Scars come physically, emotionally, and mentally. Sometimes they are the result of our own etching. Other times they come as the result of hurt inflicted by others. Regardless of the reason the scars are there, God can change your view of them. And He's the ONLY one who can transform your feelings of disgust and despair into peace and joy. He alone can deliver you from the past so you can rest and enjoy the present!

The following guidelines will help release you from yesterday's scars and set you on the firm and steady ground of Christ's love.

1. *Recognize your need for God.* We get in trouble when we try to make it on our own. Women are notorious for that! We aim toward perfection in family relationships, business endeavors, and volunteer work. We even become compulsive about our hobbies or friends. Now is a good time for you to back off! Tell your Heavenly Father you need Him more than you need anybody else.

He loves you more than anything, and He longs for a relationship with you more than anything you can do for Him!

> "Whom have I in heaven but you? And earth has nothing I desire besides you." Psalm 73:25, NIV

◯ **Put a check here if you need to work on this guideline.**

2. *Refuse to compare yourself with others.* Looking at other women who seem to have it all together is a real temptation. You may have an unhealthy perspective of trying to be like someone else. God has a unique plan for *you*. His purpose for each of His children is God-designed, and only He knows the plan He has designed for you. Spend time in His Word and expect Him to speak to you about who you are in Him.

"I know the plans I have for you, declares the LORD, plans to prosper you and not to harm you, plans to give you hope and a future."
Jeremiah 29:11, NIV

○ **Put a check here if you need to work on this guideline.**

3. *Develop godly relationships.* One of the most wonderfully beneficial and joyful things I've done as I've "matured" through the years is to latch on to a few close buddies. There's always strength in numbers! When you age with a friend, you compare notes and spur each other on. To know my friend has experienced the same struggles I face, or she has had a variation of the same difficulties, is so encouraging. Godly friendships are a gift from above!

"A man who has friends must himself be friendly."
Proverbs 18:24, NKJV

○ **Put a check here if you need to work on this guideline.**

What is God revealing to you through today's study?

_____

_____

As you close this week's study, begin by praying:

Dear Father, How I long to grow up in You! I yearn to move through each phase of life with Your grace and Your glory. Help me age in such a way that every woman younger than me will look forward to being my age! I love You.

Committing to the Lord

"Commit to the LORD whatever you do, and your plans will succeed"
(Proverbs 16:3, NIV).

This is a week for reflection, meditation, and commitment. You will be using the Scriptures, the defrazzlers, and the truths you've learned to lead you to a time of commitment to the Lord.

Coming to the end of a Bible study is difficult, isn't it? The Lord has guided us through some wonderful lessons. We've memorized Scripture and hidden it in our hearts. We've worked through the activities and defrazzlers, and we've learned new truths that have the potential to change our lives. That's a lot of stuff!

Being a former teacher, I know the value of revisiting and reviewing material after it's been presented. My prayer is that you will enjoy reflecting on the content of the last five weeks. Take plenty of time to talk with the Lord as you review. Don't try to review all five weeks in one sitting. Allow yourself a new day to process each one. Be prepared to share with your small group what the Lord is revealing to you.

Seek His direction as you make life-changing commitments that will refresh you, energize you, and equip you to better serve Him.

God bless you, my new "victoriously frazzled" sister!

Cindi Wood

Week ✿ Frazzle Friendly

1. Looking back over your notes for this week, what concept or truth most
   mpacted your life?

   _____

   _____

   _____

2. What changes have you made in your thinking and behavior as a result
   of this week's study?

   _____

   _____

   _____

3. In what ways was the defrazzler helpful?

   _____

   _____

   _____

   Is it one you will continue to practice? Why or why not?

   _____

   _____

   _____

4. Write the week's memory verse below, committing to hide it in your heart.

_____

_____

_____

5. Has God revealed anything else to you during today's review?

_____

_____

_____

Close your time in prayer, asking your Heavenly Father to bring to your mind the truths He wants you to take from this material during the days and weeks ahead.

Week 2 Control Freaks

1. Looking back over your notes for this week, what concept or truth most impacted your life?

_____

_____

_____

2. What changes have you made in your thinking and behavior as a result of this week's study?

_____

_____

_____

3. In what ways was the defrazzler helpful?

_____

_____

_____

Is it one you will continue to practice? Why or why not?

_____

_____

_____

4. Write the week's memory verse below, committing to hide it in your heart.

_____

_____

_____

5. Has God revealed anything else to you during today's review?

_____

_____

_____

Close your time in prayer, asking your Heavenly Father to bring to your mind the truths He wants you to take from this material during the days and weeks ahead.

Week ❸ Responding God's Way

1. Looking back over your notes for this week, what concept or truth most impacted your life?

_____

_____

_____

2. What changes have you made in your thinking and behavior as a result of this week's study?

_____

_____

_____

3. In what ways was the defrazzler helpful?

_____

_____

_____

Is it one you will continue to practice? Why or why not?

_____

_____

_____

4. Write the week's memory verse below, committing to hide it in your heart.

_____

_____

_____

5. Has God revealed anything else to you during today's review?

_____

_____

_____

Close your time in prayer, asking your Heavenly Father to bring to your mind the truths He wants you to take from this material during the days and weeks ahead.

Week 4 God's Practical Power

1. Looking back over your notes for this week, what concept or truth most impacted your life?

_____

_____

_____

2. What changes have you made in your thinking and behavior as a result of this week's study?

_____

_____

_____

3. In what ways was the defrazzler helpful?

_____

_____

_____

Is it one you will continue to practice? Why or why not?

_____

_____

_____

4. Write the week's memory verse below, committing to hide it in your heart.

_____

_____

_____

5. Has God revealed anything else to you during today's review?

_____

_____

_____

Close your time in prayer, asking your Heavenly Father to bring to your mind the truths He wants you to take from this material during the days and weeks ahead.

Week 5 I'm Getting Old!

1. Looking back over your notes for this week, what concept or truth most impacted your life?

_____

_____

_____

2. What changes have you made in your thinking and behavior as a result of this week's study?

_____

_____

_____

3. In what ways was the defrazzler helpful?

_____

_____

_____

Is it one you will continue to practice? Why or why not?

_____

_____

_____

4. Write the week's memory verse below, committing to hide it in your heart.

_____

_____

_____

5. Has God revealed anything else to you during today's review?

_____

_____

_____

Close your time in prayer, asking your Heavenly Father to bring to your mind the truths He wants you to take from this material during the days and weeks ahead.

❀ HOW TO BECOME A CHRISTIAN ❀

God wants us to love Him above anyone or anything else because loving Him puts everything else in life in perspective. In God we find the hope, peace, and joy that are possible only through a personal relationship with Him. Through His presence in our lives we can truly love others, because God is love.

John 3:16 says, "God loved the world in this way: He gave His One and Only Son, so that everyone who believes in Him will not perish but have eternal life." In order to live our earthly lives "to the full" (John 10:10, NIV), we must accept God's gift of love.

A relationship with God begins by admitting we are not perfect and continue to "fall short of the glory of God" (Romans 3:23, NIV). The price for these wrongdoings is separation from God. "The wages of sin is death, but the gift of God is eternal life in Christ Jesus our Lord" (Romans 6:23).

God's love comes to us right in the middle of our sin. "God proves His own love for us in that while we were still sinners Christ died for us!" (Romans 5:8). He doesn't ask us to clean up our lives first—in fact, without His help we are incapable of living by His standards.

Forgiveness begins when we admit our sin to God. When we do, He is faithful to forgive and restore our relationship with Him. "If we confess our sins, he is faithful and righteous to forgive us our sins and to cleanse us from all unrighteousness" (1 John 1:9).

Scripture confirms that this love gift and relationship with God are not just for a special few but for everyone. "Everyone who calls on the name of the Lord will be saved" (Romans 10:13). If you would like to receive God's gift of salvation, talk to Him and say:

Dear God, I know that I am imperfect and separated from You. Please forgive me of my sin and adopt me as Your child. Thank You for this gift of life through the sacrifice of Your Son. I believe Jesus died for my sins. I will live my life for You. Amen.

If you prayed this prayer for the first time, share your experience with your small-group leader, your pastor, or a trusted Christian friend. To grow in your new life in Christ, continue to cultivate this new relationship through Bible study, prayer, and fellowship with other Christians. Welcome to God's family!

Leader Guide

This leader guide will help you facilitate six small-group sessions (plus an optional introductory session) for *Victoriously Frazzled*. The optional introductory session offers a time to distribute the workbooks and get acquainted. If you choose not to have an introductory session, be sure that participants receive their workbooks in time to complete week 1 before group session 1. Announce the study in the church newsletter, worship bulletin, on hallway bulletin boards, and at women's ministry activities.

Before each session, complete each week's assignments. As the leader you do not have to have all the answers, but you need to be familiar with the material. Don't feel you have to cover every activity in this leader guide. More discussion starters are offered each week than you will be able to cover in a single session. Be flexible. Consider the personality of your group as you make decisions about which topics to discuss. Allow the Lord to lead your group discussions.

If your group is larger than 12-15 women, you may want to divide them into smaller groups for discussion. This will help participants develop more intimate relationships as the study progresses. Your small group may consist of ladies who have already completed *The Frazzled Female*—together or in other groups, ladies who have not studied *The Frazzled Female,* or a combination of the two. Make sure the ladies who have not studied *The Frazzled Female* understand it is not a prerequisite to this study. But they may want to go back and study it when they complete *Victoriously Frazzled.*

INTRODUCTORY SESSION (OPTIONAL)

Before the Session

1. Read About the Author (p. 4) and About the Study (p. 5) and be prepared to introduce the author, the study, and the format. If your group has completed *The Frazzled Female,* they will be familiar with these things and you will only need to explain the differences in the two studies.

2. Have copies of *Victoriously Frazzled* ready for distribution.

3. Prepare an attendance sheet for members to sign their names, addresses, phone numbers, and e-mail addresses. Place this sheet on a table with pens, markers, nametags (large enough for participants to draw a small picture on), and a basket for collecting money.

4. Bring markers and poster board or butcher paper for the ladies to write on. You will be posting this every week of the study, so make sure it is something you can leave hanging in your meeting room or you can take with you and bring back each week.

During the Session

1. As participants arrive, ask them to sign in and pick up copies of the member book. If group members will be paying for their own workbooks, invite them to leave payment in the basket or offer to collect their money after the session. As they prepare their nametags, ask them to draw a picture that represents what is causing the most stress in their lives right now.

2. Introduce yourself and, depending on the familiarity of the group, give a little information about yourself. Show the group members the picture you drew on your nametag and explain its meaning. Ask each member to do the same. If your group is larger than 12-15 ladies, you may want to divide into smaller groups to save time and begin to develop more intimate relationships.

3. Briefly summarize the introductory material about the author. Draw attention to the About the Study page, and take some time to explain the unique elements of the study—the Defrazzler and Relax in the Word sections. Encourage them to journal during the week about their experiences with these things, and explain that they will have an opportunity to share their experiences each week in their group session. Explain that there will also be places throughout the study where the author will ask them to journal about specific things.

4. Encourage members to share why they chose to participate in this study and what they anticipate happening in their lives as a result. If you have a group with some ladies who have completed *The Frazzled Female*, ask them to share what they learned from that study and why they are back to participate in *Victoriously Frazzled*. For participants who are new to the study, ask, *What frazzles you? How would you change your life to make it less frazzled?*

5. Remind everyone of the meeting times for each session. Emphasize the important of individual study and group participation. Remind participants that everything discussed in your group will be kept confidential.

6. Assign week 1 for the next small-group session. Encourage them to complete each learning activity to get the most out of this study.

7. Close in prayer, asking God to give you an open heart as you commit to this study.

8. As participants leave, ask them to write their names on the poster board or butcher paper you have taped to the wall. Have them write a short statement about the picture they drew on their nametags of what stresses them most. Explain that you will come back to these statements at the end of the study to see what they have learned about handling that stress.

SESSION 1

Before the Session

1. If you did not have an introductory session, prepare the attendance sheet as directed in Before the Session for the optional introductory session. Place the attendance sheet, nametags, pencils or pens, and Bibles near the door. Have member books available for newcomers.

2. Complete the week 1 material.

3. Hang the poster of names and stressors before the group session begins.

During the Session

1. As participants arrive, ask them to sign in and get their nametags. If you have newcomers, have them make nametags and then add their names and stressors to the poster.

2. If you did not have an introductory session, follow steps 1-5 in the optional introductory session suggestions. Explain that each week you will discuss the material each person had studied individually during the week. Encourage them to complete every learning activity to get the most out of their study.

3. Draw their attention to the Totally Committed page (p. 109). Read through the commitment together, and ask participants to sign the page. Take a few minutes to let them sign each other's books as they commit to support other group members during the study.

4. Recite the week's memory verse (Psalm 91:1) together.

5. Use the following discussion starters:

   a. Ask for a volunteer to read Exodus 14:14. Ask, *Are you an "Israelite" wandering around doomed to stress and forgetting God is in control and will lead you to victory?* Have participants share the battlefields they listed at the top of page 8. Discuss, *Are you ready to let God fight your battles? Do you truly believe He can and will fight your battles? Are you reluctant to give Him control of your battles?*

   b. Read Psalm 91:1, AMP (p. 10). Discuss participant's thoughts about how the author describes "the secret place." Direct them to page 11, under Why Do I Want to Go There? Ask, *Which one of the statements and Scripture promises most touched you? Why?* Remind them that it doesn't matter if they grow their intimacy with the Lord quickly or slowly. What's important is that they are growing it.

   c. Ask, *Have you ever wondered how your life got so out of balance? Were you surprised at how you responded to the activity on page 13? Is your life more balanced or less balanced than you thought?* Ask a volunteer to read Jeremiah 33:3. Remind them that Jesus intercedes for them and longs to see them live balanced, healthy, joyful lives. Read aloud, as a group, the four statements listed on page 14. Explain, *We are NOT meant to handle everybody's problems and take care of every situation!*

   d. Discuss responses to the activity on page 17—the statements that most nearly describe "where" you are in life. Ask, *Do you recognize that you do have some time to spend with Him? How do you feel when you read, "God understands our schedules. He promises that if we will give Him some time—even if we only have a little time—He will take it and multiply our blessings because we are giving to Him in love and obedience"? Does this promise make you more willing to carve out time to spend with Him?*

   e. Share, *With tragedy surrounding us at every turn—from death and serious illness to terrorist attacks and natural disasters—it's often easiest for us to assume our "minor" issues aren't important to God because there are so many "bigger" issues out there. God cares about our stresses—big and small. He wants us to come to Him about everything in our lives. When we are reluctant to do this, we tend to take more of it on ourselves leaving us unable to rest in Jesus in the midst of our daily lives.* Ask group members to share things in their lives that they have felt were too insignificant to take to God. Ask for a volunteer to read Mark 6:31.

Encourage the ladies to follow the instruction of this Scripture before it's too late and they crash from the exhaustion of trying to handle it all themselves.

6. Invite members to share their experiences with the Defrazzler and Relax in the Word assignments. If they need extra encouragement, you might want to share your experiences to get things started. As the group spends more time together, they will become more comfortable with sharing their experiences.

7. Close your time together in prayer, committing your study to God. Begin your prayer time by reading Philippians 3:10, AMP (p. 21). Ask the Lord to help you make each week's individual study and participation in each small-group session a priority.

8. Assign week 2 for the next small-group session.

SESSION 2

Before the Session

1. Complete the week 2 material.
2. Prepare the room for your small-group session. Place pencils or pens and Bibles near the door.
3. Hang the poster of names and stressors before the group session begins.

During the Session

1. Welcome the ladies as they arrive.
2. Recite the week's memory verse (Ephesians 4:2) together.
3. Use these discussion starters:
   a. Ask participants to discuss the areas in their lives they most like to control and why. Ask, *How does it feel when you aren't in control of these things?* Explain, *We do need to take control of some areas of our lives, but we spend most of our time and energy trying to control things we were never meant to control.* Ask for a volunteer to read Galatians 3:20. Remind them, *We don't have to be in control because God is!*
   b. Discuss Andrea's situation from page 26. Ask participants if they have ever experienced a similar situation in which they gave their plans completely to God and then the unexpected happened. Talk about how they reacted to the situation. Share, *When we've committed our plans to the Lord in prayer and have done our best to carry them through, we often can't believe it when things go wrong. When these situations come, the Lord isn't trying to rattle us. He's trying to lead us to trust Him no matter how things appear.* Read Proverbs 3:5-6 as a reminder of Who is really running the show.

    c. Have participants talk about people or situations in their lives with which they have had an either/or relationship. Ask, *What do you think causes you to have these control urges? What steps can you take to turn these things over to the Lord and get more balance in your life?*

    d. Ask for a volunteer to read Galatians 5:22-23. Explain, *God begins to develop self-control in you as soon as the Holy Spirit takes up residence in your heart. You don't have to muster it up, but you do have to stop, think, and appropriate the power of Christ instead of reacting from your own natural tendencies.* Refer to the activity on page 34 about exercising self-control. Ask participants to share which guideline poses the greatest challenge for them and why.

    e. Share, *On day 5 we learned about dealing with others who try to control. Think of controllers you know—don't call names! Which of the fears listed on page 36 do you think are most likely behind their need to control? How does recognizing these fears and motivations change how you will react to these people? Understanding the reasons others need to control situations may also help us understand why we try to control things ourselves.*

4. Invite the ladies to share their experiences with the Defrazzler and Relax in the Word assignments. If they need some extra encouragement, share your experiences to get things started.

5. Close your time together in prayer. Ask the Lord to help you recognize areas where you need to take control, as well as areas where you need to release control.

6. Assign week 3 for the next small-group session.

SESSION 3

Before the Session

1. Complete the week 3 material.
2. Prepare the room for your small-group session. Place pencils or pens and Bibles near the door.
3. Have markers or chalk and a chalkboard, poster board, or flip chart available.
4. Hang the poster of names and stressors before the group session begins.

During the Session

1. Welcome the ladies as they arrive.
2. Recite the week's memory verse (Matthew 7:12) together.
3. Use these discussion starters:

a. Ask volunteers to give their definitions of *reacting* and *responding*. Write their answers on the board or flip chart. Ask, *What things cause you to react rather than respond? What factors contribute to your reaction?* Ask someone to recall the answer the author gave for how we learn to respond rather than react [we plan to]. Discuss things you can do to develop that plan and respond with love and gentleness, just like Jesus.

b. Say, *In day 2 the author states: "If we don't think before we respond, and if we don't train ourselves to be like Christ, then we won't be like Him and we won't respond like Him. We need reminders placed in our paths to help us remember our goal."* Ask for volunteers to share reminders they have used in the past or plan on using in the future to help them remember to respond like Christ. Encourage group members to find an accountability partner if they don't already have one. Remind them that they need someone who will encourage them and hold them accountable, someone with whom they can share their concerns and vulnerabilities.

c. Read 2 Corinthians 3:18. Talk with group members about how easy it is to react in the flesh when things are hectic. Say, *The Lord wants to transform us, but we have to cooperate with His plan.* Ask volunteers to share what commitments they made to cooperate with God's plan in the activity on page 47. Ask everyone to stop and write down some specific steps they will take to meet their commitments.

d. Ask group members to share stories of when they were caught off guard by someone who snapped at them. Ask them to also share how they reacted or responded. If they reacted in a less than positive manner, ask for ideas of what they could have done to "heap coals." Spend several minutes in silent prayer. Instruct participants, *Talk to the Lord about a past situation that you handled poorly. Ask Him to show you what you can do now regarding that situation to share His love and bring honor to His name.*

e. Share, *We have just completed our third week of* Victoriously Frazzled! *One thing we have learned is that intimacy with God brings godly reactions, and intimacy with God comes from spending time with Him and getting to know Him. Let's take some time to share victories we have experienced as a result of knowing Him better.* Ask group members to share a recent incident when they reacted graciously in a situation that they would not have normally handled well. Encourage everyone to come up with one—no matter how big or small. It's important for them to recognize the changes they are making.

4. Invite the ladies to share their experiences with the Defrazzler and Relax in the Word assignments. If they need some extra encouragement, share your experiences to get things started.
5. Close your time together in prayer. Ask the Lord to help you react and respond to people and situations in ways that glorify Him.
6. Assign week 4 for the next small-group session.

SESSION 4

Before the Session
1. Complete the week 4 material.
2. Prepare the room for your small-group session. Place pencils or pens and Bibles near the door.
3. Have markers or chalk and a chalkboard, poster board, or flip chart available.
4. Hang the poster of names and stressors before the group session begins.

During the Session
1. Welcome the ladies as they arrive.
2. Recite the week's memory verse (Mark 6:31) together.
3. Use these discussion starters:
   a. Ask for a show of hands, *How many of you have come through a period of feeling distant from God? How many of you are feeling distant from God now?* Ask those who have come through a period of feeling distant from God to share with those who are currently experiencing the distance how they responded, what steps they took to reclaim the nearness they once felt, and what they learned through the process. Encourage those who are currently feeling distant from God to take the advice Eli gave Samuel in 1 Samuel 3:9. Remind group members, *God loves you and is pursuing a love relationship with you. And He wants you to hear His voice and welcome Him into your daily life of places to go, things to do, and people to take care of.*
   b. Say, *On day 2, the author shares that her family members each keep a portion of an x-ray taken after her son was in a serious car accident. Each small clipping serves as a "monument of victory" to remind them of God's intervention. Do you have something that serves as a "monument of victory" in your life?* Ask volunteers to share about their remembrances and how they help them remember what God has done in their lives.

    c. Read John 14:16 (AMP) and list on the board the names given to the Holy Spirit in this passage [Counselor, Helper, Intercessor, Advocate, Strengthener, Standby]. Ask group members to come up and list situations in their lives where they need His guidance through these specific roles. Explain that they don't have to have an answer for each one, but they can contribute to as many as they like. After everyone has had a chance to contribute, discuss the answers.

    d. Pick a well-known praise chorus everyone will know and sing it as a group. Direct everyone to page 65 and recite Philippians 4:13 together. Ask group members how they feel about singing and reciting praise to God in this way. Ask for ideas of how people use verbal praise in their own personal quiet time with God.

    e. Discuss Leslie's story from the beginning of day 5. Ask group members if they can identify with Leslie. Say, *On page 68 the author shares the checklist she uses as a guideline to follow in her quiet time with the Lord. Page 69 was provided for you to make your own checklist. What things did you list—what activities you would like to include in your quiet time? What habits would you like to develop?* If they need help coming up with ideas, refer them to the list on page 67.

4. Invite the ladies to share their experiences with the Defrazzler and Relax in the Word assignments.

5. Close your time together in prayer. Thank the Lord for the times He has intervened in your life, for the opportunity to praise Him, and for the opportunity to grow closer and closer to Him. Tell Him how much you love Him.

6. Assign week 5 for the next small-group session.

SESSION 5

Before the Session
1. Complete the week 5 material.
2. Prepare the room for your small-group session. Place pencils or pens and Bibles near the door.
3. Hang the poster of names and stressors before the group session begins.

During the Session
1. Welcome the ladies as they arrive.
2. Recite the week's memory verse (Isaiah 46:4) together.
3. Use these discussion starters:

a. Ask participants to name good things about getting older. Explain, *One of the best things about getting older is being able to use experiences from our lives to help others who are experiencing the same things.* Refer to the list of life experiences on page 73. Ask group members to share opportunities they have had to share specific life experiences (positive or negative) with younger women walking the same paths. Ask, *How did it feel to help someone else learn from your life?*

b. Explain, *Finding a healthy balance with things like eating and exercise can be difficult. Many times it becomes all or nothing. How we care for ourselves directly affects our self-esteem.* Ask volunteers to share which balance strategy they picked from page 75 to focus on and why. Remind group members that we were created in the image of God and He wants us to find a healthy balance in taking care of our bodies.

c. Ask someone to share about an older person who has influenced her with his or her positive attitude. Ask another group member to share about a young person she knows who is making an impact for Jesus. Ask someone else to share about a person in middle or older years who has inspired her with his or her usefulness to God. Say, *These people remind us that we can have a positive influence on others at any age, but sometimes we're still bothered by the fact that we're getting older.* Ask participants which Scripture promise listed on page 79 encourages them most about getting older and why.

d. Read Matthew 7:17. Ask, *Are you bearing good fruit or bad fruit?* Remind group members of the author's observation that there is no mention of the age of the tree in this passage—because it doesn't matter! Say, *We are called to bear good fruit at every age of life. What are some excuses you have used for not enjoying life and bearing fruit? What problem do you see with those excuses now?*

e. Ask, *Is there something you would like to be that you never got to be, something you would like to do that you never got to do?* Have fun with this! The things they mention will probably be light-hearted and fun in nature, but it's likely that every lady in the room has at least one serious regret from her past. Explain, *We all have regrets from things we have done or left undone, but those things are in the past. There's no reason to hang on to yesterday's moments, we can't relive or redo.* Draw group members' attention to the three guidelines to help release yesterday's scars listed on pages 84-85. Ask if anyone chose guideline 1 as the one she needed to work on. Ask her to read Psalm 73:25 and share why she chose this guideline. Ask for someone who picked guideline 2 to read Jeremiah 29:11 and share why she chose this guideline. Ask for someone who picked guideline 3 to read Proverbs 18:24 and share why she chose this guideline.

4. Invite the ladies to share their experiences with the Defrazzler and Relax in the Word assignments.
5. Close your time together in prayer. Thank the Lord for the opportunity to grow older with Him. Thank Him for creating you in His image and for the assurance that He will use you at ANY age.
6. Assign week 6 for the next small-group session. Point out that this week of study will be different because there is no study content. This will be a week for reflection, meditation, and commitment. Encourage group members to read the message from the author on page 86 and prayerfully approach the week with the expectation that the Lord will reveal new things to them.
7. Discuss having a *Victoriously Frazzled* party to celebrate the end of your Bible study and the victories you have experienced during your time together. If you decide to have a party, make a plan for participants to bring snacks and other needed items.

SESSION 6

Before the Session
1. Complete week 6.
2. Prepare the room for your small-group session. Place pencils or pens and Bibles near the door.
3. Make any necessary preparations for your *Victoriously Frazzled* Party.
4. Hang the poster of names and stressors before the group session begins.

During the Session
1. Welcome the ladies as they arrive.
2. Ask all participants who are willing to share one thing the Lord revealed to them during this week of reflection and commitment. Encourage everyone to share, and remind them that the Lord may want to use their experiences to speak to others in the group.
3. Call the ladies' attention to the poster of names and stressors they created during the first small-group session. Ask them to share where they are with those stressors now. Celebrate the victories together. Pray with those who are still struggling.

4. Take the rest of your group time to party and celebrate being "victoriously frazzled" women. Talk about next steps for your group. If the group wants to continue together with another Bible study, talk about options for things to study next. No matter what your group plans for the future, commit to pray for each other as you continue to face the daily assaults of the world.

5. Close your time together in prayer. Thank the Lord for the opportunity to study together and develop relationships with other women. Ask for His continued strength as you face life in a stress-filled world.

Totally Committed

I, _____, commit to my
Father, my Bible study partners, and myself to:

1. Love the Lord with all my heart, soul, and mind.
2. Seek first His kingdom during the next six weeks.
3. Complete the weekly assignments before each group meeting.
4. Pray for the women in my group.
5. Keep the confidential matters discussed within the group session confidential.
6. Be open and obedient to the Holy Spirit's promptings.

Signature: _____

Signatures of group members:

_____

_____

_____

_____

_____

_____

_____

_____

Getting a handle on life is an inside job!

If *Victoriously Frazzled* was your introduction to discovering the peace and joy the Lord desires for you in spite of the stresses of life, check out *The Frazzled Female!*

This six-week study is packed with many of the same components you experienced in this study. Each week includes a Defrazzler to help you experience more deeply the concept you are studying that week. The Weekend Mini-Retreat is an optional time of study designed to help you go deeper with the Lord. The book of John is the focus for these times.

Dive into Scripture with The Frazzled Female, actively and creatively applying God's Word to your daily life!

To order this resource (item 0-6330-9526-5): WRITE LifeWay Church Resources Customer Service; One LifeWay Plaza; Nashville, TN 37234-0113; FAX order to (615) 251-5933; PHONE (800) 458-2772; ORDER ONLINE at *www.lifeway.com*; or VISIT the LifeWay Christian Store serving you.